CHARACTER CAKES

CHARACTER

SANDY GARFIELD

GUILD PUBLISHING LONDON

In memory of my father,
who would have been tickled pink

This edition published 1989 by Guild Publishing
by arrangement with Sidgwick & Jackson Limited

Reprinted 1989

CN 1028

Produced by the Justin Knowles Publishing Group
9 Colleton Crescent, Exeter, Devon, EX2 4BY

Design: Ron Pickless

Home economist: Amy Awan
Illustrations: Antonia Enthoven
Photography: Charles Parsons, Focus Photography, Exeter

Typeset by Scribes, Exeter
Printed by Printer Industria Grafica, Barcelona

CONTENTS

INTRODUCTION

Every parent knows that no children's party, birthday or otherwise, is complete without a cake – it is the *pièce de résistance*. These days children are demanding ever-more ambitious creations and I know that many parents rack their brains trying to come up with something new and surprising. I hope that this book will go a long way towards solving their problem.

In the following pages you will find instructions on how to recreate many of your children's favourite characters in edible form. Some of the cakes are trickier to make than others, so begin with one of the simpler designs to practise using fondant, icings, and food colours. Progress on to the sculpted cakes when you are feeling more confident.

All the cakes are fun to make and even more fun to eat. Don't strive for perfection and, if you run out of time or patience, do improvise with chocolates, sweets, and biscuits as alternative decorations.

You'll find that it will not only be children who love your works of art – adults, too, will want Character Cakes for their own birthdays.

BASIC CAKE AND ICING RECIPES

NOTES AND HANDY HINTS

The recipes I have suggested here are those that I find to be easy to work with and to produce the most delicious cakes. But you can, if you wish, use any of your own favourite recipes. Provided that the cakes are firm and adequately cooled you should have no problems.

You should aim to make any cake at least three hours before you want to use it to create your Character Cake. Never cut or sculpt a cake that has just been taken out of the oven as it may crumble. If you prefer, you can bake the cake well in advance and keep it in the freezer until you need it.

I have not included a recipe for a fruit cake, because so many people prefer to use their own tried and tested personal versions, but any of the Character Cakes may be made with fruit cake. In fact, fruit cakes are excellent for sculpting. They will also keep for weeks if covered with fondant icing.

Two words of advice to help you produce more nearly perfect cakes. When you scoop the cake mixture into the tin ready for baking, spread it out and level the top with a metal tablespoon dipped in hot water. This prevents the top of the cake exploding and cracking like a volcano. And when you take the cooked cake out of the oven, leave it in its tin to cool for about 10 minutes before turning it out on to a wire rack. Otherwise it may still crack and crumble and be difficult to work.

You can make the small round cakes (for Mickey Mouse's ears, for example) either in the 4in (10cm) round individual pie tins available at most good hardware stores or in any suitably sized round oven-proof dishes you may have, remembering to grease them well first.

In all the recipes you may, if you wish, use soft margarine instead of butter – for economy and to give a rather milder taste.

Here is a check list of the pieces of kitchen equipment you will need for your cake making. Obviously, you will not use every item to make every cake. Read the recipe first to see what you should have ready.

12in × 10in (30cm × 25cm) cake tin
9in (22.5cm) square cake tin
8in (20cm) round cake tin
4in (10cm) diameter round cake tins (or oven-proof dishes)
2pt (1l) oven-proof earthenware or glass pudding basin
measuring jug or flower pot
baking sheets
greaseproof paper
measuring spoons
measuring cup
kitchen scales
flour sifter
sieve
egg whisk
lemon grater
lemon squeezer
wooden spoon
mixing bowl
metal spoon
skewer
wire cake rack
cake board
small saucepan
palette knife
sharp knife
pastry brush
storage jars (for glazes)
polythene bags (for storage of fondant and marzipan)

In all the recipes, quantities are given in both Imperial and metric measures. Because the conversions cannot be exact, use one set of measures only when following the recipes. All spoon measures are level – a teaspoonful is taken to be 5ml.

MADEIRA CAKE

Madeira is an excellent cake for cutting into shapes or sculpting as it will not crumble when cut.

Ingredients

| | Quantities for | | | | |
	12in × 10in (30cm × tin)	9in (22.5cm) square tin	8in (20cm) round tin	2pt (1l) pudding basin	2 4in (10cm) round tins
self-raising flour	14oz ( )	12oz (340g)	10oz (285g)	6oz (170g)	2oz (60g)
plain flour	7oz (200g)	6oz (170g)	5oz (140g)	3oz (85g)	1oz (30g)
butter	14oz (395g)	12oz (340g)	10oz (285g)	6oz (170g)	2oz (60g)
caster sugar	14oz (395g)	12oz (340g)	10oz (285g)	6oz (170g)	2oz (60g)
eggs	7	6	5	3	1
grated rind and juice of orange or lemon	2½	2	2	1	½
approximate cooking time	1hr 40mins	1hr 30mins	1hr 20mins	1hr 15mins	30mins

Method

1 Grease the tin and line it with greaseproof paper.
2 Sift the flours together.
3 Cream together the butter and sugar until the mixture is light and fluffy.
4 Beat in the eggs one at a time, alternating with spoonfuls of flour.
5 Fold in the remaining flour.
6 Add the grated rind and the juice of the orange or lemon.
7 Put the mixture into the tin and place in a preheated oven at 160°C (325°F), Gas mark 3.
8 Bake for the approximate time shown above, until the cake is firm to the touch and a skewer inserted into its centre comes out clean.

SPONGE CAKE

This is lighter and fluffier than the Madeira cake, but it will not keep as long, so bake and decorate it as near as possible to the day on which it will be eaten. It tastes wonderful.

Ingredients

| | Quantities for | | | | |
	12in × 10in (30cm × 25cm) tin	9in (22.5cm) square tin	8in (20cm) round tin	2pt (1l) pudding basin	2 4in (10cm) round tins
self-raising flour	12oz (340g)	8oz (225g)	7oz (200g)	6oz (170g)	3oz (85g)
baking powder	2½tsp (12.5ml)	2tsp (10ml)	2tsp (10ml)	1½tsp (7.5ml)	1tsp (5ml)
cornflour	3oz (85g)	2oz (60g)	1oz (30g)	2tsp (10ml)	1tsp (5ml)
butter	14oz (395g)	10oz (285g)	8oz (225g)	6oz (170g)	3oz (85g)
caster sugar	13oz (370g)	9oz (255g)	7oz (200g)	5oz (140g)	2oz (60g)
vanilla essence	10 drops	10 drops	8 drops	6 drops	3 drops
eggs	7	5	4	3	1
approximate cooking time	60mins	60mins	50–60mins	50–60mins	30mins

Method

1 Grease the tin and line it with greaseproof paper.
2 Sift together the flour, baking powder, and cornflour.
3 Cream together the butter and sugar until the mixture is light and fluffy and add the vanilla essence.
4 Beat in the eggs one at a time, alternating with spoonfuls of flour.
5 Put the mixture into the tin and place in a preheated oven at 160°C (325°F), Gas mark 3.
6 Bake for the approximate time shown above, until the cake is firm to the touch and a skewer inserted into its centre comes out clean.

Alternative flavours
Chocolate: substitute for the cornflour the same amount of cocoa powder and omit the vanilla essence.
Coffee: omit the vanilla essence and add – to the 7-egg mix, 3tbs (45ml) coffee essence or 6tbs (90ml) instant coffee powder; to the 5-egg mix, 2½tbs (37.5ml) coffee essence or 5tbs (75ml) instant coffee powder; to the 4-egg mix, 2tbs (30ml) coffee essence or 4tbs (60ml) instant coffee powder; to the 3-egg mix, 1½tbs (22.5ml) coffee essence or 1tbs (15ml) instant coffee powder; to the 1-egg mix, ½tbs (7.5ml) coffee essence or ½tbs (7.5ml) instant coffee powder.
Orange or lemon: omit the vanilla essence and add – to the 7-egg mix, 7tsp (35ml) grated orange or lemon rind and 2tbs (30ml) juice; to the 5-egg mix, 5tsp (25ml) grated orange or lemon rind and 2tbs (30ml) juice; to the 4-egg mix, 4tsp (20ml) grated orange or lemon rind and 1tbs (15ml) juice; to the 3-egg mix, 3tsp (15ml) grated orange or lemon rind and 1tbs (15ml) juice; to the 1-egg mix, 1tsp (5ml) grated orange or lemon rind and ½tbs (7.5ml) juice.

CHOCOLATE CAKE

This rich, moist chocolate cake is delightfully quick and simple to make.

Ingredients

	12in × 10in (30cm × 25cm) tin	9in (22.5cm) square tin	8in (20cm) round tin	2pt (1l) pudding basin	2 4in (10cm) round tins
plain flour	16oz (450g)	12oz (340g)	10oz (285g)	6oz (170g)	3oz (85g)
bicarbonate of soda	1½tsp (7.5ml)	1tsp (5ml)	1tsp (5ml)	½tsp (2.5ml)	pinch
baking powder	3tsp (15ml)	2tsp (10ml)	1½tsp (7.5ml)	1tsp (5ml)	pinch
cocoa powder	4tbs (60ml)	3tbs (45ml)	2tbs (30ml)	1½tbs (22.5ml)	1tbs (15ml)
soft brown sugar	10oz (285g)	7oz (200g)	6oz (170g)	4oz (115g)	2oz (60g)
butter	7oz (200g)	5oz (140g)	4oz (115g)	2oz (60g)	1oz (30g)
milk	1¼ cup (355ml)	1 cup (285ml)	¾ cup (215ml)	½ cup (140ml)	¼ cup (70ml)
golden syrup	4tbs (60ml)	3tbs (45ml)	2tbs (30ml)	1½tbs (22.5ml)	1tbs (15ml)
eggs	4	3	2	1	1
approximate cooking time	50–60mins	50–60mins	50–60mins	50–60mins	25–30mins

Method

1 Grease the tin and line it with greaseproof paper.
2 Sift the flour, soda, baking powder, and cocoa into a mixing bowl, and stir in the sugar.
3 Put the butter and milk into a small saucepan and place over a very gentle heat until the butter has melted.
4 Add the syrup, eggs, melted butter, and milk to the bowl of dry ingredients and with a wooden spoon beat the mixture to a smooth batter.
5 Pour the mixture into the tin and place in a preheated oven at 160°C (325°F), Gas mark 3.
6 Bake for the approximate time shown above, until the cake is firm to the touch and a skewer inserted into its centre comes out clean.

APRICOT GLAZE

Use apricot glaze before icing a cake with fondant or royal icing or giving it a layer of marzipan. It will prevent any crumbs getting into the icing. There is no need to use glaze before applying butter icing. Apricot glaze is also useful for sticking pieces of cake together and for mending any breakages.

Ingredients
8oz (225g) apricot jam
2tbs (30ml) water

Method
1 Put the jam and water in a saucepan and heat gently until the jam has melted.
2 Bring to the boil and simmer until thick.
3 Strain the mixture through a sieve and discard the pulp.
4 Pour into a clean jar and store in the refrigerator until required. (It should keep for about a month, but boil it again and let it cool before you use it.)
5 Apply the glaze to the cake with a small pastry brush.

MARZIPAN

Marzipan may always be used to cover the top of a cake before fondant or royal icing is applied. Remember to brush the cake with apricot glaze first.

It is also handy for filling any holes you may find when you turn a cake upside down for icing. It is an excellent material for moulding and sculpting cakes such as The Snowman and for forming little figures of people or animals.

Marzipan can be bought ready-made, but it is easy to make your own. This recipe is for white marzipan, which you should use when you need to end up with a coloured marzipan – yellow marzipan (made with egg yolks) does not take colour well. The quantities given here will make 1lb (450g).

Ingredients
4oz (115g) icing sugar
4oz (115g) caster sugar
4oz (115g) ground almonds
2 egg whites
4 drops almond essence
1tsp (5ml) lemon juice

Method
1 Sift the icing sugar and mix together the sugars and the ground almonds.
2 Add the beaten egg whites, almond essence, and lemon juice and mix the whole lot together to form a stiff but manageable dough.
3 Turn on to a surface sprinkled with icing sugar and cornflour and knead until smooth. Be careful not to overdo the kneading or the marzipan will become too oily.
4 Wrap the paste in polythene or keep it in an airtight container until it is needed.

ROYAL ICING

In place of the egg whites called for by this recipe you can instead use egg albumen powder, which is available from specialist cake-decorating shops. It is easy to use and it disposes of the problem of using up the egg yolks. Always use egg albumen powder for making small amounts of royal icing – measuring out half an egg white is tricky!

This recipe is for 8oz (225g) of royal icing.

Ingredients
1 egg white
8oz (225g) icing sugar
1tsp (5ml) lemon juice
a few drops of glycerine (optional)

Method
1 Beat the egg white until it is frothy, then gradually beat in half the well-sifted icing sugar. Continue beating until the mixture is smooth and white. Add the lemon juice. Then slowly beat in enough of the remaining icing sugar to give the correct consistency – the mixture should be firm enough to stand up in little peaks.
2 If you prefer a softer consistency, add a little glycerine, drop by drop, with the lemon juice. Be careful not to overdo it, though, or the icing will be too soft to handle.
3 Put the icing into an airtight container, or in a bowl covered with a damp cloth. Leave it to stand for a while, until air bubbles come to the surface and burst. Then it is ready to use.
4 Royal icing can be stored in an airtight container for up to two days before use. Stir it thoroughly and add a little more sifted icing sugar if necessary.

To make small amounts
Make a paste of ½tsp (2.5ml) egg albumen powder and 1tbs (15ml) water. Sift about 4oz (115g) icing sugar and add it to the paste, a spoonful at a time, until the mixture forms peaks.

Run-outs
Run-outs are small shapes made with royal icing thinned down with lemon juice or water to make it easy to spread.

Trace the shape you are going to make on to a sheet of greaseproof paper. You can, if you wish, pipe round the outline with some thinned icing through a no.1 or no.2 nozzle, but this is not always necessary. Fill the centre of the shape with a teaspoonful or so of thinned icing and spread it carefully out to the edges of the shape with the end of a teaspoon. Gently tap the surface of the board you are using to level the icing.

Always make two or three extra shapes, to make up for any failures. Leave the run-outs for at least 24 hours to dry. They can then be kept in an airtight container until you are ready to use them. Peel off the greaseproof paper very carefully, by pulling it downwards away from the shape. Treat the run-outs gently – they are very fragile.

FONDANT ICING

Fondant is an extremely versatile and cooperative icing. With it you can cover cakes of all shapes and sizes. You can cut out any number of different patterns from it. You can colour it with liquid or paste food colours. You can leave it white and paint on it with a brush.

Ready-made fondant icing can be bought from most supermarkets, but some makes tend to be rather greasy. You can bring them to a less sticky consistency by kneading in some sifted icing sugar.

Always roll out fondant icing on a board sprinkled with a mixture of icing sugar and cornflour, otherwise the fondant icing will stick to the board and be unworkable. The same mix of icing sugar and cornflour can also be used to disguise any small cracks and slight imperfections in the fondant – rub it into the icing with small circular movements of the fingertips for best results.

This recipe for do-it-yourself fondant icing makes 1lb (450g).

Ingredients
1lb (450g) icing sugar
1 egg white
2oz (55g) liquid glucose (obtainable from chemists)

Method
1 Thoroughly sift the icing sugar, put it into a bowl, and make a well in its centre.
2 Add the egg white and liquid glucose.
3 Beat all the ingredients together with a wooden spoon, scooping up all the icing sugar from the edges of the bowl.
4 Knead the mixture in your hands, with some extra icing sugar to prevent it sticking. When it is soft and smooth, wrap it in a polythene bag and store it in a cool place until required. Knead it again just before you use it.

Clear glaze
If you want a truly professional look, you can make this clear glaze to help put a wonderful gloss on your fondant. It is especially effective for making fondant eyes shine.

Simply mix together 1tbs (15ml) gum arabic powder (obtainable from specialist cake shops or from chemists) with 3–4tbs (50ml) water and stir over boiling water until the powder has dissolved. Strain the glaze through a sieve and store in a jar until required.

TRAGACANTH FONDANT

A limitation of ordinary fondant is that it will crack and tear if you try to fold it, so if you want to achieve an effect of, for example, rippling cloth you should use tragacanth fondant. This is quite satisfactory on its own, but I have found through experimenting that the best results are gained by using a mixture of equal amounts of tragacanth and ordinary fondant kneaded together.

Ingredients
2tsp (10ml) gelatine
1tbs (15ml) water
1tbs (15ml) gum tragacanth (obtainable from specialist cake shops or chemists)
¾lb (340g) icing sugar
2tsp (10ml) liquid glucose
1 egg white

Method

1 Soak the gelatine for 5 minutes in the cold water.

2 Sift the gum tragacanth and about half the icing sugar into a bowl, and make a well in the centre.

3 Add the glucose to the gelatine and melt them together over hot water.

4 Whisk the egg white until stiff.

5 Add the egg white and gelatine and glucose mixture to the icing sugar and stir very carefully with a wooden spoon.

6 Knead the mixture well, with some extra icing sugar to prevent it sticking to your hands.

Tragacanth icing, in a polythene bag, will keep in the refrigerator until required. Knead it again before you use it.

BUTTER ICING

Butter icing can be coloured and flavoured, used as a piped decoration or spread to cover an entire cake. To achieve a smooth finish when icing a cake, spread the butter icing with a small palette knife. Keep a jug of hot water beside you and dip the palette knife into it frequently. Keep on spreading and smoothing the butter icing in this way until you are happy with the finish.

This recipe makes 8oz (225g) of butter icing. If the instructions for a Character Cake call for less than that amount, either reduce the ingredients proportionately or make the full amount and store any surplus until it is needed.

Ingredients

4oz (115g) butter
8oz (225g) icing sugar
1tbs (15ml) golden syrup (optional)
a few drops of vanilla essence
1–2tbs (25ml) milk

Method

1 Cream the butter until pale and soft. Continue beating, adding the sifted icing sugar a little at a time. Add in, too, the golden syrup if you wish (it tastes wonderful – try it!).

2 Add the vanilla essence to the mixture and as much of the milk as is necessary to give a smooth spreading consistency.

Butter icing, stored in an airtight container, will keep for up to a week in the refrigerator. Leave it out until it reaches room temperature before you use it. It may also be frozen, but must be thawed thoroughly before use.

Alternative flavours

Chocolate: substitute for the vanilla essence 1–2tbs (25ml) cocoa powder dissolved in a little hot water or 1½oz (45g) melted plain chocolate.

Coffee: omit the vanilla essence and either beat in 1tbs (15ml) instant coffee powder or substitute coffee essence for the milk.

Orange or lemon: omit the vanilla essence and use, instead of the milk, the juice and the grated rind of half a lemon or orange.

THE CHARACTERS

NOTES AND HANDY HINTS

Read each recipe through before starting and make sure you have all the necessary tools and ingredients handy. Where several differently coloured fondants will be used, colour them all in advance and keep them wrapped in polythene or cling film to prevent them drying out.

Character Cakes using butter icing should ideally be made on the day they are to be eaten, because butter icing goes hard if left too long. At earliest, they should be made only the day before they are to be eaten. Fondant-iced cakes can be made several days in advance, because fondant preserves the cake beneath. Never freeze any cake that has coloured icing – the colours will run when the cake thaws.

Some recipes specify levelling off the top of the cake and turning it upside down. This is to provide a flat and even surface to work on. You may find that once the cake is upturned some small gaps remain at what is now the bottom. Fill these in by kneading small pieces of marzipan in your hands and pushing them under the cake where necessary (Fig. 1). Cut off any excess with a sharp knife (Fig. 2).

Before icing a cake with fondant, first apply a coat of apricot glaze or a layer of marzipan, or both. Then roll out the fondant on a surface liberally sprinkled with sifted icing sugar and cornflour. Always use a rolling pin to lift a large, rolled-out piece of fondant on to the top of a cake (Fig. 3). Use your fingertips to press the fondant over the top and down the sides of the cake (Fig. 4), and trim off any surplus with a sharp knife. Disguise any cracks or other imperfections by rubbing a mixture of sifted icing sugar and cornflour over the surface with your fingertips, in small circular movements.

2 Cut off the excess with a sharp knife.

1 Push small pieces of marzipan into the gaps under the cake.

3 Use a rolling pin to lift a large, rolled-out piece of fondant onto the top of a cake.

4 Use your fingertips to press fondant over the top of the cake and down the sides.

You may have some fondant left over when the cake is finished. It need not be wasted. Knead it into a ball and keep it for another time in an airtight polythene bag. Knead it again before you use it. Similarly, you are bound to have bits and pieces of cake left over. You can make a quick trifle with them by pressing them into a bowl, adding some sherry and fruit, and topping with cream.

You may use either liquid or paste food colourings for the fondant. Add the colouring to the fondant in drops from the end of a skewer. Knead it in with your fingertips until the colour you want is reached. Always add the colour little by little – it is easy to make the fondant darker, but tricky to make it paler. If you overdo it, though, the simplest solution is to knead a piece of white fondant into the coloured fondant to lighten it.

It is easier to paint on to fondant if it has been allowed to dry for a few hours. A food pen will make dents in fresh, soft fondant. But it is not difficult to paint on to fresh fondant with a brush if you are really pressed for time.

When a recipe requires one piece of fondant to be laid on top of another, dip a small paintbrush into a cup of water and dampen one of the pieces very slightly. Fondant sticks well to itself when just damp.

You will need cake boards to make your Character Cakes. A wide variety can be bought in department stores, specialist cake shops, and stationers. They will be limited, though, to square or circular boards in either gold or silver. Try making your own from thick cardboard or by covering a kitchen chopping board with a colourful wrapping paper. Glue or pin a piece of paper cut to size and shape to the surface of the board. Use coloured tape to cover the sides. If the paper you use is absorbent, cover it with the self-adhesive film you can buy to protect book covers. This will prevent the paper soaking up butter from the cake and becoming marred by unsightly grease marks.

You will need a few sheets of tracing or greaseproof paper, a ruler, and a felt-tip pen to copy the patterns from the templates provided here for the Character Cakes. Each square in the grids used in this book represents in full scale a 1in (2.5cm) square. To make a pattern for a cake, you should first rule a 9in × 9in (22.5cm × 22.5cm) square for a 9in (22.5cm) cake, or a 12in × 10in (30cm × 25cm) rectangle for a rectangular cake of that size, and so on. Divide this into 1in (2.5cm) squares. Copy the drawing from the book, working from square to square. Some drawings are more complicated than others, so try some of the simpler ones first to get used to the process.

You will use the drawings just like dressmakers' patterns to cut shapes, not in material, but in fondant and cake. To form a cake from a template, cut round the outline and fix the cut-out shape to the top of the cake with dressmakers' pins. Then cut round the outline with a sharp knife. Remove the template and keep it beside you for reference while you work. Keep several spare pieces of tracing paper handy, because you may need to cut out separate templates for parts of the cake.

Other items of equipment you will need are:

a selection of sharp knives
pastry brush
rolling pin
measuring spoons
small paint brush
food-colouring pens
icing bag and nozzles
cocktail sticks
tweezers
wire cake rack
polythene bags (to store fondant)

MICKEY MOUSE

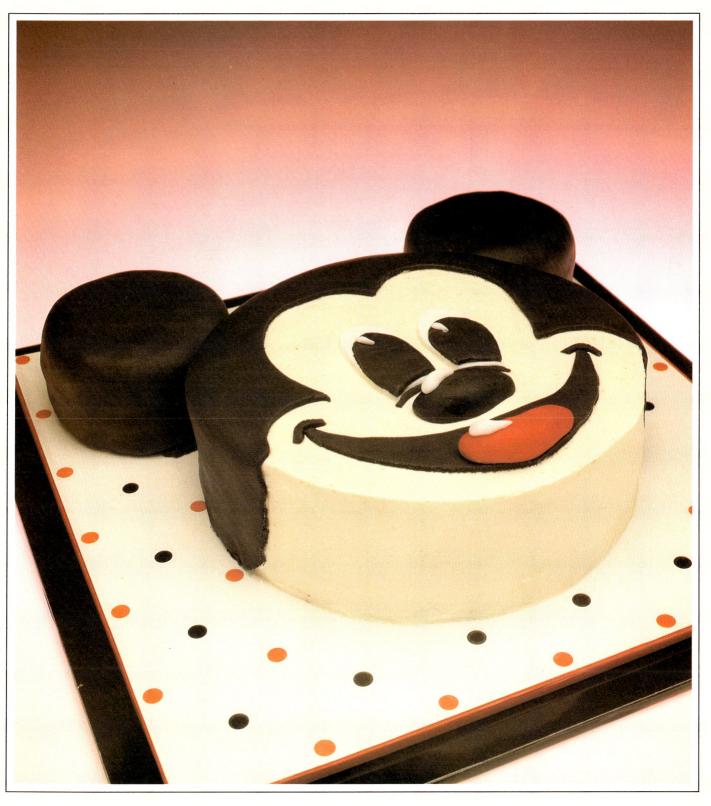

This cake is fairly simple and great fun to make. I have allowed for extra fondant to overlap the sides of the ears and the hair, but if you want to make it even easier just cut the fondant to fit the top of the cake and leave the sides covered in butter icing.

You will need
1 8in (20cm) round cake for his face
2 4in (10cm) round cakes for his ears
8oz (225g) butter icing
apricot glaze
10oz (285g) fondant: pinch of red; pinch of white; remainder black
food-colouring pastes: black and red

Method
1 To make the ears, sandwich two of the small round cakes together with butter icing. Brush all over with apricot glaze.
2 Cover the sides and the top of the face cake with butter icing. Make the join as neat as you can.

3 Roll out the black fondant and place the hair template in the centre. Cut round the inner hairline, but leave a border of at least 2in (5cm) round the outside to cover the sides of the cake (Fig. 1). Place the fondant hairpiece on the cake as shown in the photograph.
4 Gather up the excess fondant, knead it and roll it out again. Cut two large circles (approximately 7in (18cm) in diameter) to cover each ear. Using a template, cut out the mouth, and place it on the cake. Mould an oval shaped nose by rolling a piece of fondant in the palms of your hands, and place this on the cake.
5 Cut out two eye pieces from white fondant, and stick two slightly smaller pieces of black fondant on top. Place them on cake above the nose.
6 Mould red fondant into the shape of the tongue, as shown in the photograph, and press on to mouth.
7 Make tiny balls of white fondant into highlights and place on the eyes, nose and mouth. Cut a really thin strip of black and place it just below the eyes. Place the ears in position next to head.

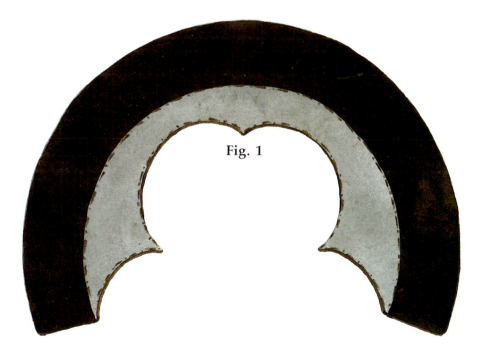

Fig. 1

DONALD DUCK

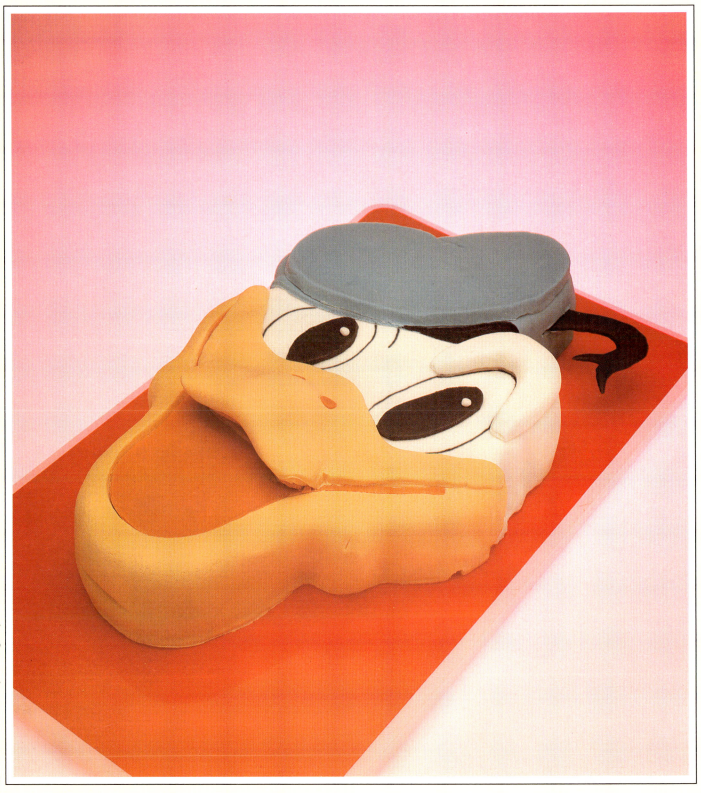

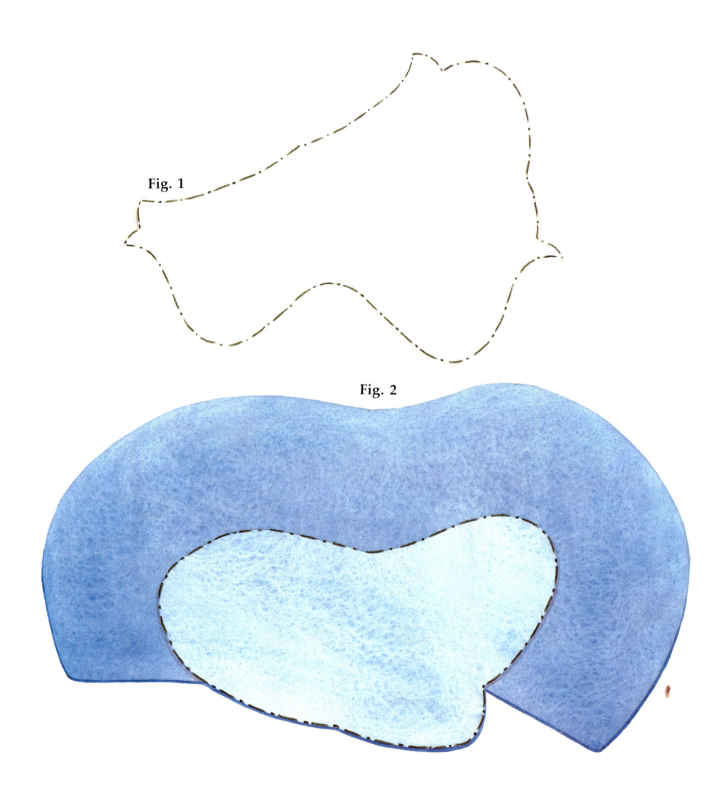

Fig. 1

Fig. 2

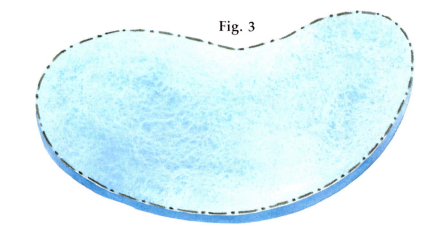

Fig. 3

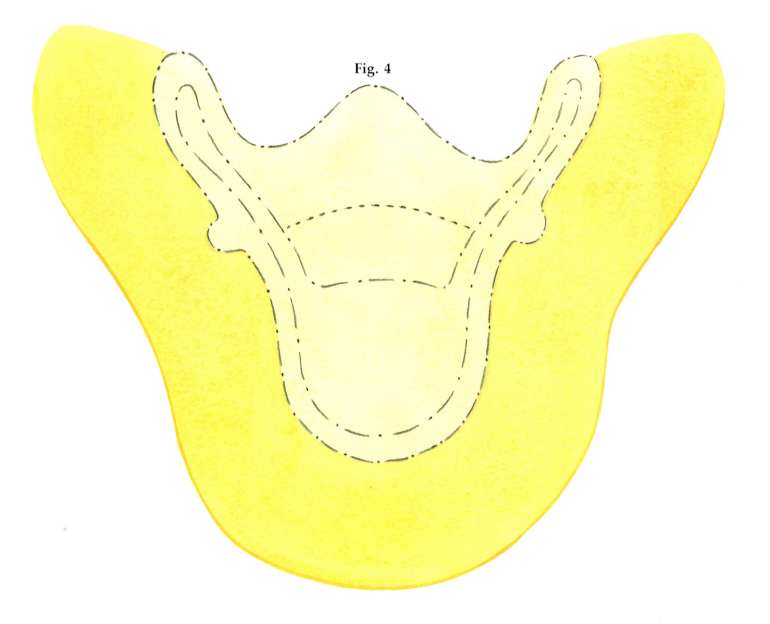

Fig. 4

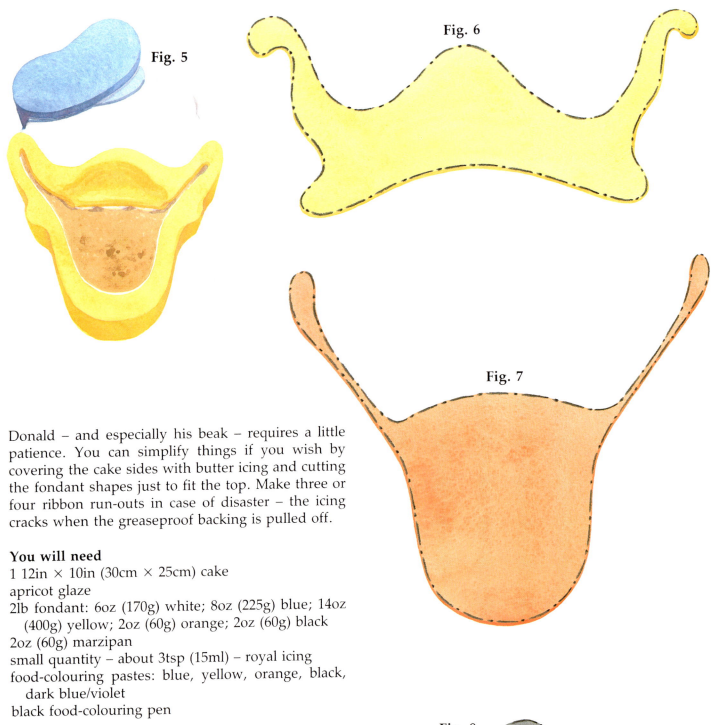

Fig. 5

Fig. 6

Fig. 7

Donald – and especially his beak – requires a little patience. You can simplify things if you wish by covering the cake sides with butter icing and cutting the fondant shapes just to fit the top. Make three or four ribbon run-outs in case of disaster – the icing cracks when the greaseproof backing is pulled off.

You will need
1 12in × 10in (30cm × 25cm) cake
apricot glaze
2lb fondant: 6oz (170g) white; 8oz (225g) blue; 14oz (400g) yellow; 2oz (60g) orange; 2oz (60g) black
2oz (60g) marzipan
small quantity – about 3tsp (15ml) – royal icing
food-colouring pastes: blue, yellow, orange, black, dark blue/violet
black food-colouring pen

Method
1 You will need two templates of Donald's head. From one cut the cake to shape, and brush it all over with apricot glaze. Cut the second into pieces representing the white face, yellow beak and blue hat.
2 Roll out white fondant and place the face template in centre. Cut out the two longest sides, but leave

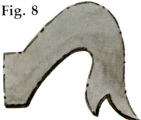

Fig. 8

about 2½in (6cm) strips attached to the ends to cover the sides of the cake (Fig. 1). Lift on to cake, smooth down the sides, and trim.

3 Roll out blue fondant. Place hat template in centre. Cut round bottom edge of hat where it joins the face, but leave a good border to cover sides of cake (Fig. 2). Lift on to cake, smooth, and trim.

4 Knead together pieces of surplus blue fondant and roll out again. Cut out a slightly smaller hat shape traced from your original drawing and stick it on top of the first hat (Fig. 3).

5 Cut a small slit at the side of the hat to take the royal-icing ribbon later. Cut out a template of the basic beak shape and place in centre of rolled-out yellow fondant. Cut round top edge but again leave a border for the sides of the cake (Fig. 4). Lift carefully over a rolling pin and place in position on cake. Press down sides and trim.

6 With a small sharp knife cut out a mouth shape on the yellow fondant and carefully peel it off the cake (Fig. 5).

7 Knead some lumps of marzipan into small balls and put them aside.

8 Lift up the end of the beak with the back of a spoon and gently fold the end under. Try to mould the curved corners of the beak as you go. Hold the beak open and quickly press two or three lumps of marzipan under the beak to support it. Let go of the beak and let it rest on top of the marzipan.

9 Knead surplus yellow fondant and roll out again. Using the original template, trace and cut out the shape of the top beak only (Fig. 6). Place it on fondant and cut round it. Brush the back of it with a little water and gently press it on top of the first, rolled-back, beak. Mould the two together to give a rounded appearance and curve the lower edge under to give a neat finish. This is quite tricky, but use the photograph as a guide.

10 Roll out the orange fondant. Trace a rough mouth shape from the original drawing. Place it over the fondant and cut out (Fig. 7). It is a good idea to test all your fondant shapes first by using rough tracing-paper shapes placed in position on the cake. Then you can adjust the sizes if necessary. Lift the mouth piece into position on the cake, making sure it fits well under the beak. Make two small dents on top of the beak and fill them with two tiny balls of orange fondant.

11 Take a small piece of white fondant and shape it into an eyebrow. Brush it with water on the underside and position on the face.

12 Roll out black fondant and, using templates, cut out the eye shapes. Brush with water and position on cake. Then draw round the eyes with a black food colouring pen.

13 To complete Donald's head, you need to make the ribbon. First of all, mix up some food colouring to give a dark blue. I used blue and violet together to get a good strong colour. Using a small paintbrush, paint a little strip of blue directly on to the blue fondant at the base of the hat. Mix the royal icing with the food colouring. Make the ribbon run-out by tracing the shape (Fig. 8) on to a piece of greaseproof paper and using the method described on page 11. Leave to dry for at least 24 hours and very gently push into the slot at the side of the hat.

DUMBO

Here is Disney's little elephant who learned to fly and his drum. The drum cake is easy to make but Dumbo himself needs extra care. Try making him from Madeira cake as it has the firmest consistency for the tricky bits – cutting out his trunk and standing him up. Proceed slowly and cautiously.

You will need, for Dumbo

1 9in (22.5cm) square cake
apricot glaze
6oz (170g) fondant: a pinch of white; remainder grey
6oz (170g) butter icing
food-colouring pastes: black, blue and pink

Method

1 Turn cake upside down and cut it into the shape of the little elephant, using a template (Fig.1). Be especially careful when cutting round the trunk, which is quite narrow. Use a small, very sharp knife to make it easier.

2 Brush all over the cake with apricot glaze. Roll out the grey fondant and, using the template, cut from it the same elephant shape. Lift it on to the cake, again being extra careful with the trunk (Fig.2).

3 Gather up surplus fondant, knead again, and roll out. Cut out an ear and a small tail and stick in place with a little water. Curl up the edges with your fingertips (Fig. 3).

4 Make an eye with a pinch of white fondant. When it has dried out a little, paint on the blue iris and black pupil. Also paint on to the cake an eyebrow and lines to indicate the leg, knee, and trunk creases. Make little toes from white fondant and stick these in place.

5 If you are feeling adventurous you can colour the butter icing pink and spread it over the sides of the cake. This may prove tricky when you come to lift Dumbo upright onto the drum, but you can always smooth the sides again when he is upright. Do not spread butter icing under his feet or he may slip over. You can leave Dumbo at this stage while you go on to make the drum.

You will need, for the drum

1 8in (20cm) round cake
4oz (115g) marzipan
apricot glaze
6oz (170g) pink fondant
2 packets Smarties (or other sweets)

Method

1 Level off top of cake. Shave the sides to an angle to form a drum shape (Fig.4), Knead the marzipan

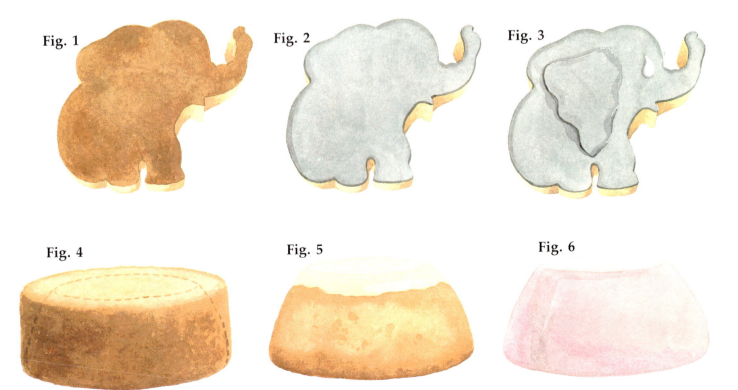

Fig. 1   Fig. 2   Fig. 3

Fig. 4   Fig. 5   Fig. 6

until soft, roll out, and cut a small circle to place on top of the cake to make it slightly higher (Fig. 5).
2 Brush all over with apricot glaze.
3 Roll out the fondant and cut out a circle large enough to cover the cake. Lift it into position with the help of a rolling pin and cut off any surplus (Fig. 6).

4 Press Smarties (or any sweets you choose) into the sides of the fondant – they will stick more firmly if you damp the fondant first with a small paintbrush.
5 Now, very carefully, lift Dumbo on to the drum and leave him sitting happily there.

TOM & JERRY

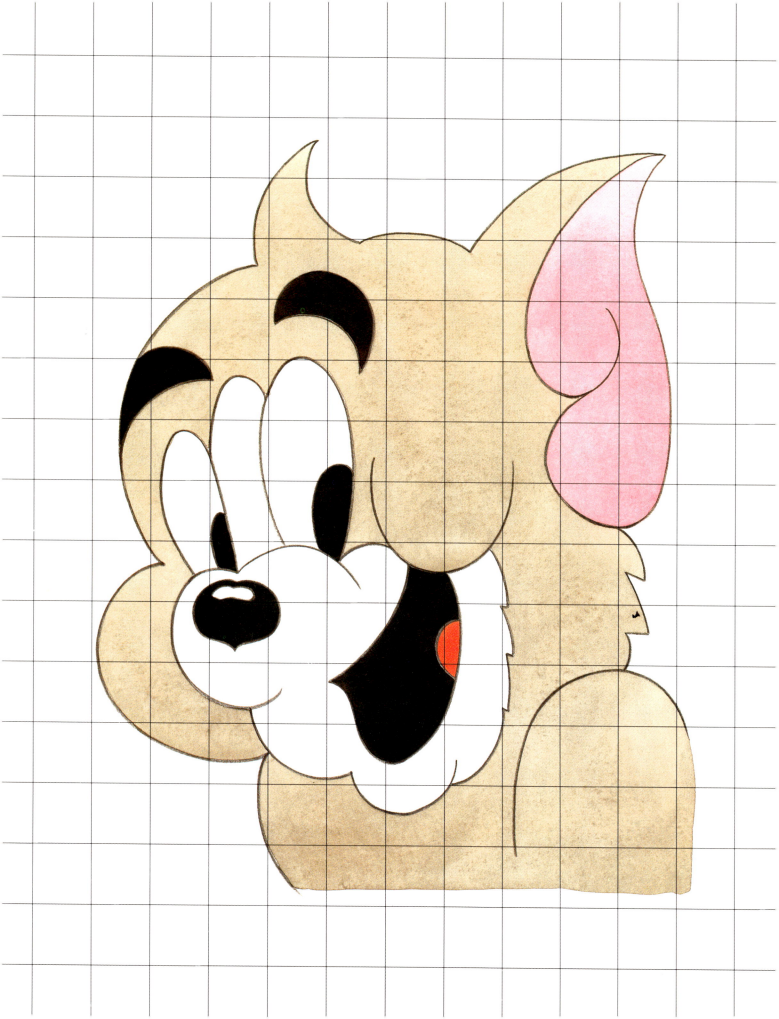

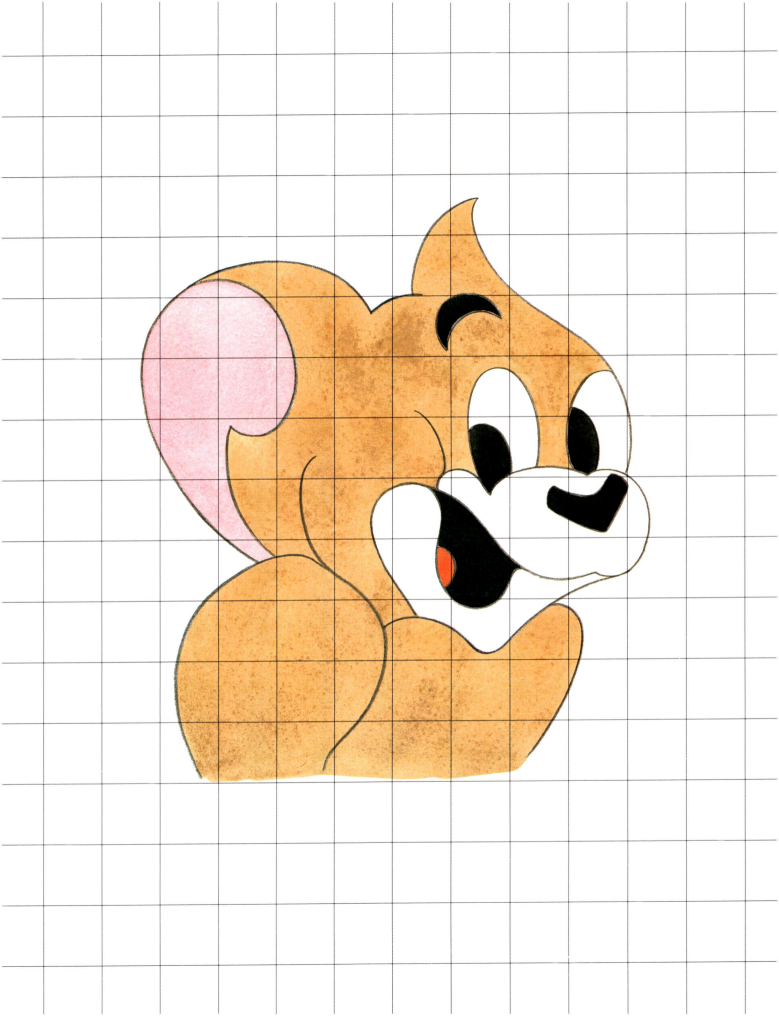

The famous cat and mouse both have good, solid shapes, without fiddly bits, that are easy to cut from a cake. To achieve a furry effect, use a fork or flat knife to peak the royal icing – but work fast, it dries out surprisingly quickly.

You will need, for Tom

1 12in × 10in (30cm × 25cm) cake
apricot glaze
1lb 8oz (680g) royal icing
1lb (450g) fondant: 7oz (200g) white; 4oz (115g) black; 4oz (115g) pink; pinch of red
a few strands of spaghetti
food-colouring pastes: black, pink, red, and (optional) violet

Method

1 Level off cake if necessary and turn upside down. Using a traced template, cut round Tom's outline and place the cake on a board. Brush the cake with apricot glaze.

2 Cut out separate templates of his face and ear. It is a good idea to cut out two of each – one set to be positioned on top of the cake and kept in place with pins (Fig. 1) and the other to be kept for cutting out fondant.

3 Colour the royal icing grey with some black food colour. (Try adding a little violet as well to give it more depth of colour.) Spread it on to the sides and top of the cake, right up to the edges of the templates. Use a fork or knife to give the icing a round, furry finish while still wet.

4 Roll out the white fondant and cut out Tom's face from the second template. Remove the template on the cake and replace it with the fondant face. Knead together any surplus white fondant and mould a round white nose (see photograph). Stick it on top of the face with a little water.

5 Cut out an ear from pink fondant and, again, position it in place of traced template.

6 Roll a blob of black fondant into a small ball to finish off the tip of the nose. Roll out some more black fondant and cut out two eyes, two eyebrows, and a mouth. Stick in position. Make some tiny strips of fondant to indicate a cheek and shoulder.

7 Make a pinch of red fondant into a tongue and stick it on the mouth.

8 Make some highlights for his eyes and nose from white fondant. Paint on the outline of the eyes in black (see photograph).

9 Finally, break off some strands of spaghetti, paint them black, and push them into Tom's cheeks.

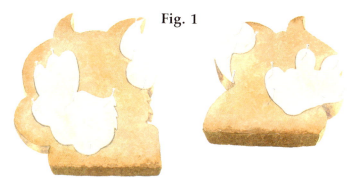

Fig. 1

You will need, for Jerry

1 9in (22.5cm) square cake
apricot glaze
1lb (450g) royal icing
15oz (425g) fondant: 6oz (170g) white; 4oz (115g) black; 4oz (115g) pink; pinch of red
a few strands of spaghetti
food-colouring pastes: black, pink, red, and chestnut brown

Method

Proceed in exactly the same way as for Tom, but colour the royal icing chestnut brown instead of grey.

POPEYE

'I yam what I yam!' Here is my favourite, spinach-loving sailor, complete with pipe. He is quite simple to make and will take shape quickly.

You will need
1 12in × 10in (30cm × 25cm) cake
apricot glaze
1lb 6oz (625g) fondant: 12oz (340g) flesh colour; 8oz (225g) white; pinch of black; pinch of brown
chocolate finger
liquorice strands (optional)
food-colouring pastes: flesh, black, and brown

Method
1 Pin a template of Popeye's face onto the flat surface of the cake and cut to shape.
2 Place cake on your board. Brush all over with apricot glaze.
3 Cut template into two along the join between head and cap. Roll out flesh-coloured fondant and place template in the centre. Cut round the top of the forehead but leave a border of about 2in (5cm) around the rest of the template to allow for the sides of the cake (Fig. 1). Lift fondant on to the cake, easing it over the sides and smoothing it down with your fingertips. Cut off excess, and keep it in a polythene bag until you need it again. Similarly, cut out the hat from white fondant and ease into position. The cake will now be covered in fondant (Fig. 2).
4 Roll out a small strip of black fondant for the cap ribbon and stick it on top of the white fondant. Make an extra piece of white fondant into the peak of the cap and stick down with a little water on the lower edge. Gently curl the top of the peak in and towards you (Fig. 3).
5 Place Popeye's face template gently back on the cake and prick through the outline of his ear, eye, eyebrows, mouth and nose with a pin. Remove the template and lightly draw in the features with either a food colouring pen or a small paintbrush (Fig. 3).
6 Make a small eye and mouth from black fondant and stick in position. Using left-over flesh fondant, make a bulbous nose, an ear, and lips. Make eyebrows from black fondant or liquorice.
7 For the pipe, first push a chocolate finger into the cake. Then, mould a bowl from a small piece of brown fondant and push it onto the end of the finger. If it is too heavy, simply use another small piece of brown fondant to support the pipe from below.

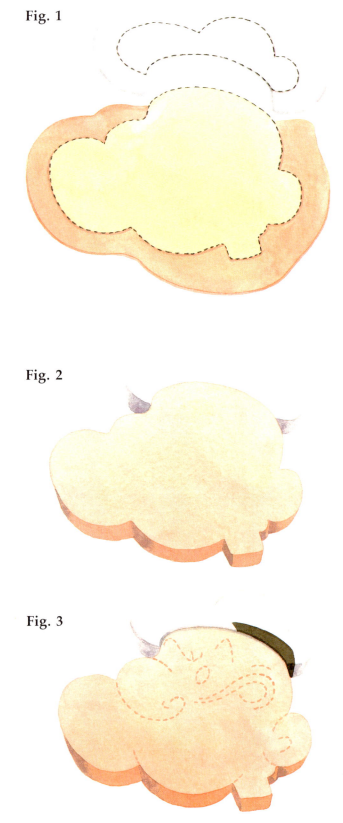

Fig. 1

Fig. 2

Fig. 3

DENNIS THE MENACE

Born in the *Beano* in 1951, this naughty schoolboy is still going strong. It is a simple cake to make, but make sure it has been well chilled before you cut it – the spikes of his hair may break off if the cake is too fresh and soft.

You will need

1 12in × 10in (30cm × 25cm) cake
apricot glaze
14oz (400g) fondant: 4oz (115g) flesh colour; 4oz (115g) black; 6oz (170g) red
4oz (115g) royal icing
8oz (225g) butter icing
food-colouring pastes: flesh, black, and red

Method

1 Turn cake upside down. Cut round Dennis's outline from a traced template.
2 Brush with apricot glaze the area of cake where Dennis's face and jumper will go.
3 Roll out flesh-coloured fondant. Using another template, cut from fondant his face, including his ears. Place it carefully in position on top of the cake.

4 Make a small ball of flesh-coloured fondant for his nose and stick it in place with a little water. Make two more ear shapes with thick round edges and stick these on top of his face.
5 Roll out the red fondant and cut out his jumper from another template. Stick it in place on the cake below his face.
6 Roll out the black fondant and cut out curved strips about 1in (2.5cm) wide. Use tracings if you wish. Stick these over the red fondant jumper.
7 Colour the royal icing black. Gently fork it over the rest of the top of the cake to make his hair.
8 Colour the butter icing to imitate flesh and spread it over the edges of the cake with a small palette knife, dipped in hot water.
9 Finally, paint a cheeky face on top of the fondant with a small paintbrush and black food colouring.

In the photograph of the Dennis the Menace cake the hair and jumper are a little different from the D. C. Thomson & Co Ltd preferred style. However, to ensure that the cake you make is as authentic as possible you should make every effort to match the shape and decoration of your cake with the template.

SUPERMAN

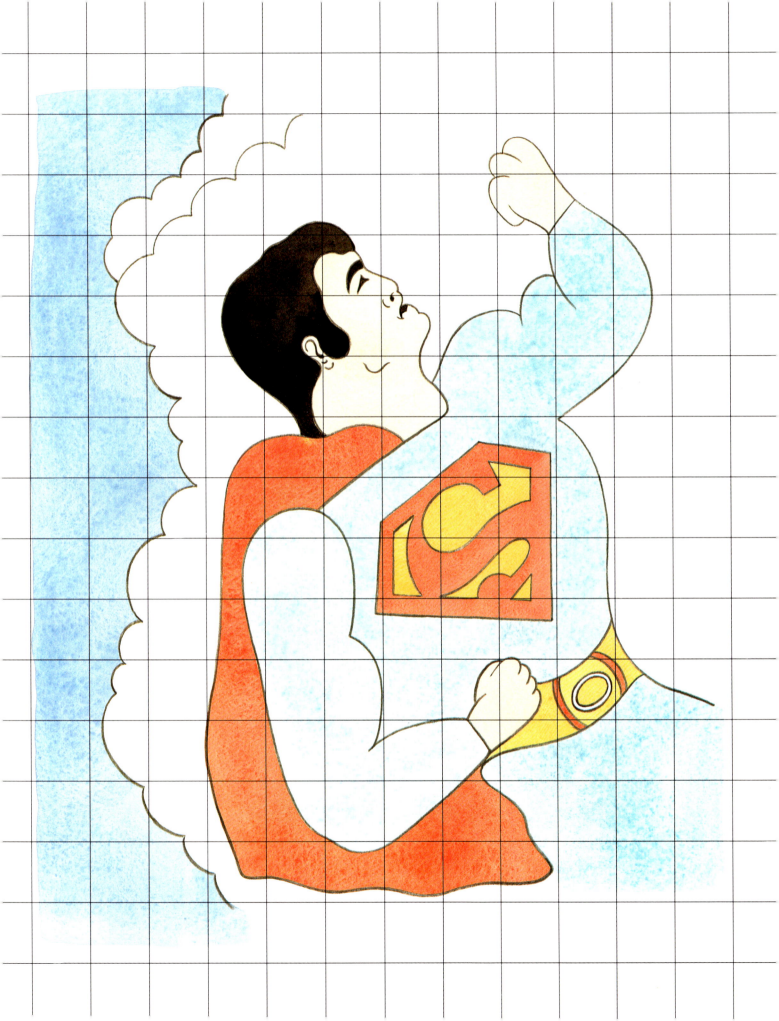

Superman is made by fitting together flat pieces of fondant rather like a jigsaw. Paint any design you choose on the white part of the cake, or write on a birthday message to make it more personal.

You will need

1 12in × 10in (30cm × 25cm) cake

apricot glaze

2lb 8oz (1.1kg) fondant: 1lb 10oz (740g) white; 7oz (200g) blue; 3oz (85g) flesh colour; 4oz (115g) red; or use half-and-half mix of ordinary fondant with tragacanth fondant

8oz (225g) royal icing

food-colouring pastes: blue, red, yellow, flesh colour, and black

Method

1 Turn the cake upside down on your board and brush the whole of it with apricot glaze.

2 Roll out the white fondant and cover the top of the cake with it. Gather up trimmings of fondant and knead them together – you will need them later.

3 Roll out the blue fondant and, using a template, cut from it Superman's body, including his arms. You will need a second upper arm.

4 Brush some water over the top of the cake in roughly the position the blue body will go. Carefully lift the blue fondant on to the cake and place in position. Take the second arm shape and place it over the first, again using some brushed-on water, to raise the arm slightly (see photograph).

5 From a separate template, cut the head from rolled-out flesh-coloured fondant and place in position next to body. Cut out two small hands from flesh fondant and make small indentations with back of knife to indicate fingers. Brush with water and stick in place.

6 Cut the Superman logo from rolled-out white fondant and place in position on his chest. Prick through the template to draw the 'S' shape on the fondant. Draw through pinpricks with a black food pen. Cut out belt and place in position.

7 When fondant has dried out slightly (1 hour minimum), you can paint in his hairline, eyes, eyebrows, nose, and mouth with a tiny paintbrush dipped in black paste. Or use a colouring pen if you prefer. Use the photograph to guide you. Paint the belt yellow and also fill in the yellow bits of the logo. Wait for a while before painting in the red 'S' and red belt straps.

8 To make his cloak, use the red fondant, or tragacanth and ordinary fondant mixture. Cut out the cloak shape, making it slightly oversize by leaving a border of about ½in (1.25cm) around the template. This is so that you can make some folds in the cloak. Lift the cloak into position on the cake and carefully fold it around Superman. This is tricky, but worth the effort because it will give the appearance of billowing in the wind! Let it overlap the side of the cake, too.

9 Paint some clouds in black on the top of the cake, again with a tiny brush or pen. Then paint in the sky in blue.

10 For his hair, colour a small amount of royal icing black and fork it on to his head. Or, if you prefer, you can simply paint it on with black colouring paste.

11 For the final decoration, colour the rest of the royal icing red and pipe a line around the base of the cake.

BATMAN

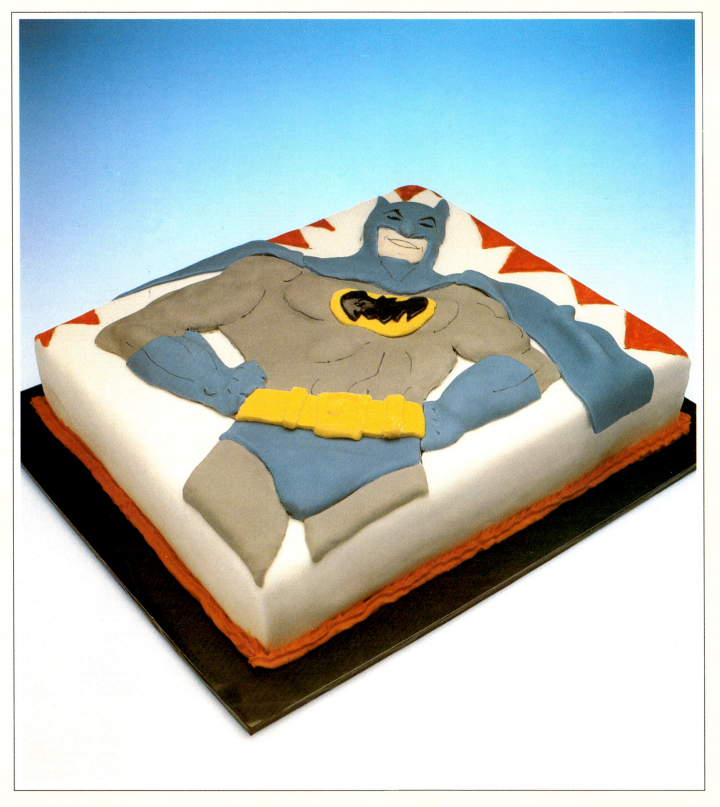

You can make an easier version of this cake by omitting the marzipan muscles and simply using flat pieces of fondant. However, it is fun to make a well-developed, muscular Batman, so be as creative as you like with the marzipan muscles.

You will need

1 12in × 10in (30cm × 25cm) cake
apricot glaze
3lb (1.35kg) fondant: 1lb 10oz (735g) white; 8oz (225g) grey; 8oz (225g) blue; 3oz (85g) yellow; pinch of flesh colour; pinch of black
6oz (170g) marzipan
8oz (225g) royal icing (optional)
food-colouring pastes: black, blue, yellow, and flesh
black food-colouring pen

Method

1 Turn the cake upside down and brush with apricot glaze.

2 Knead and roll out the white fondant and ice the whole cake with it.

3 Make a template of Batman's body and pin it in place on the cake (Fig. 1). Draw lightly round the tracing with a food pen and prick through the lines indicating his muscles. Remove the template and sketch in the muscles as well (Fig. 2).

4 Knead small pieces of marzipan until soft and, using the outline on the cake as a guide, mould the marzipan into shapes resembling muscles – it doesn't really matter how accurate you are as long as you give the body some bulk. Make a piece for his face, too (Fig. 3).

5 Cut out another template of the body and legs. Roll out the grey fondant and cut out the shapes from the templates. Ease into position over the marzipan (Fig. 4). Cut out a small face from flesh fondant by the same method.

6 Continue in the same way and cut out the hood from blue fondant, leaving a void where the face shows through. Then make two pieces of fondant into a billowing cape and fold them over Batman's shoulders and over the sides of the cake. And don't forget the famous blue pants (Fig. 5). Keep unused

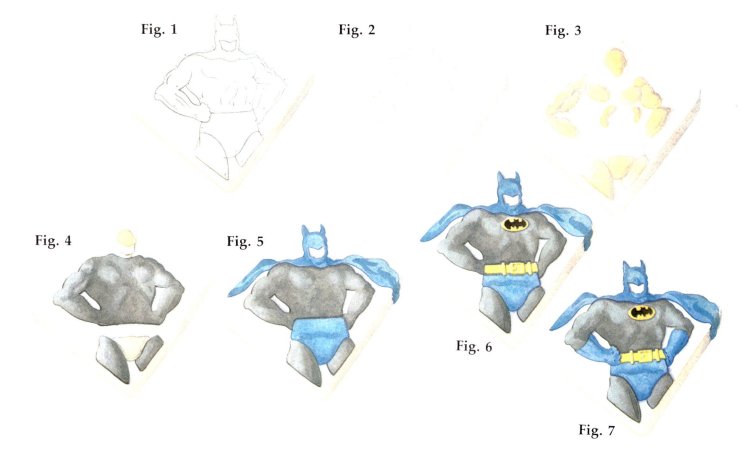

Fig. 1　　Fig. 2　　Fig. 3

Fig. 4　　Fig. 5　　Fig. 6

Fig. 7

blue fondant in a plastic bag until you are ready to make the gloves.

7 Make a belt from yellow fondant and stick down over the top of the blue pants. Add a buckle and two loops. Then cut an oval shape for the chest logo (Fig. 6).

8 Cut out the bat from black fondant and stick in position.

9 Using traced templates, make the two gloves from blue fondant and stick over the grey pieces already on the cake (Fig. 7).

10 With the paintbrush and black food colour paint in Batman's eyes, eyebrows, and mouth and emphasize the muscles on his chest and arms.

11 For a final touch, paint a design on the white part of the cake and, if you wish, pipe a border of coloured royal icing around the base.

M.A.S.K.

These two masks belong to two characters from the cartoon and comic *M.A.S.K.* The round blue mask is that of Matt Trakker, hero of the Mobile Armoured Strike Command. The angular green mask is that of Gorey, who is one of the Venom team opposing Matt and his men.

You will need, for Matt Trakker's mask

1 pudding-basin cake
1 8in (20cm) round cake
apricot glaze
2lb (900g) fondant: 10oz (285g) white; 10oz (285g) blue; 2oz (60g) green; 10oz (285g) red
1lb (450g) marzipan
food-colouring pastes: blue, green, and red
silver sugared balls

Method

1 Split the 8in (20cm) round cake in two. Using a small plate of about 7in (18cm) diameter, cut one of the halves into a smaller circle. Place it on top of the larger half. With a sharp knife, shave the pudding-basin cake into a smooth hemisphere, adding some marzipan to the top to round it off and a circle of marzipan to the base to raise it slightly. Place this hemisphere on top of the two circles (Fig. 1). Now dismantle the pieces – because each has to be covered separately.

2 Place the 8in (20cm) circle on your board and spread some apricot glaze over it. Cut out an 8in (20cm) circle of white fondant and place it over the top of the cake. Smooth down with your fingertips. Gather up the trimmings and knead again. Place the smaller cake on top, brush it with apricot glaze, and cover it with a 7in (18cm) circle of white fondant (Fig. 2).

3 Brush the pudding-basin cake with apricot glaze. Roll out the blue fondant and lift it over the cake. Press it into position and trim the surplus. Place on top of the two circles (Fig. 3).

4 With a small, sharp knife, carefully cut out a small section of blue fondant from the front of the cake. You will find it will peel off quite easily (Fig. 4).

5 Pinch off about 3oz (85g) of marzipan and knead it until soft. Then gently press it into the space where the cake is exposed and form it into a shape roughly resembling a visor (Fig. 5).

6 Cover the marzipan with two small pieces of white fondant and a piece of pale green fondant (Fig. 6).

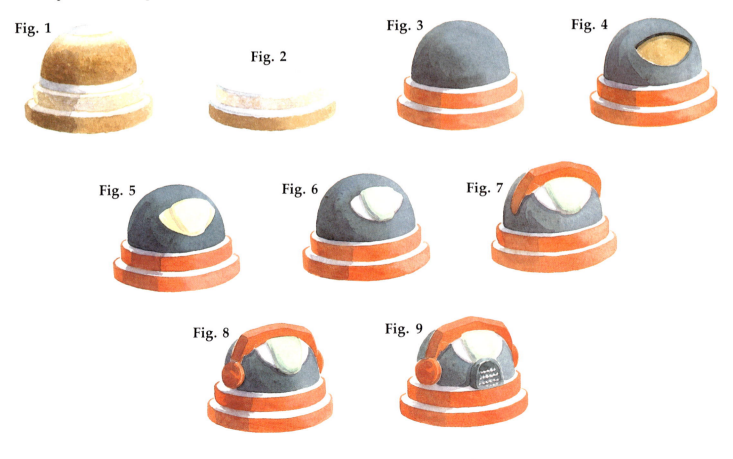

Fig. 1   Fig. 2   Fig. 3   Fig. 4

Fig. 5   Fig. 6   Fig. 7

Fig. 8   Fig. 9

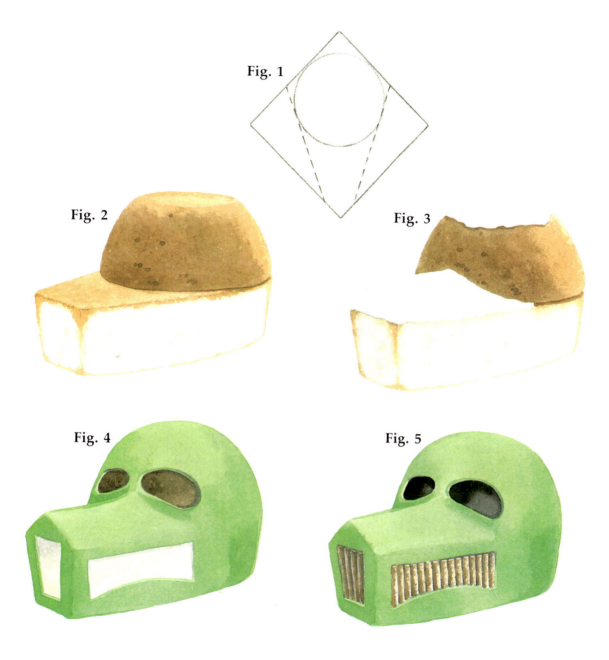

Fig. 1

Fig. 2

Fig. 3

Fig. 4

Fig. 5

(To obtain the correct shapes, experiment first with pieces of greaseproof paper.)

7 Measure off about 7oz (200g) of red fondant. Roll it out and cut into long strips that will wrap around the sides of the circular cakes (Fig. 7).

8 Knead the remaining red fondant together with any remaining marzipan, adding more colour if necessary. Roll out into a long sausage shape and cut into three pieces that will fit along the top and sides of the visor. Shape the pieces carefully with a knife into a squarer shape and place in position. Then gently mould all the pieces together until they form one section (Fig. 7).

9 With the left-over fondant/marzipan mixture make two round earphones and roll out a strip to form a strap to join them together at the back of the helmet. Press in position (Fig. 8).

10 Finally, mould a piece of blue fondant into a mouthpiece and press on to the front of the cake. Decorate with small silver balls (Fig. 9). (Make tiny dents in the fondant with the end of a teaspoon to help the balls stay in place.)

You will need, for Gorey's mask

1 pudding-basin cake

1 9in (22.5cm) square cake

apricot glaze

8oz (225g) marzipan

1lb 8oz (680g) fondant: 1lb 6oz (625g) green; 2oz (60g)
    black

a few chocolate sticks

2 chocolate biscuits

food-colouring pastes: green and black

icing sugar (optional)

Method

1 Turn square cake upside down and place the pudding-basin cake on top of it in one corner (Fig. 1). Cut the square cake as shown and trim and round off the corners to match the shape of the pudding-basin cake. Place the two cakes on your board, sandwiched together with apricot glaze (Fig. 2).

2 Knead the marzipan until soft and, using a small piece at a time, round off the top of the pudding-basin cake. Then shape the lower cake to make it more angular (Fig. 3).

3 Brush all over the two cakes with apricot glaze. Roll out the green fondant until it is large enough to cover the mask and carefully lift it over the cake, using a rolling pin to help you. Quickly smooth the fondant down with your fingertips and cut off any surplus. Then, with a small, sharp knife, cut out two eye pieces from the top of the mask and three panels from the lower part. You will find that the fondant peels away quite easily revealing the cake underneath (Fig. 4).

4 Roll out the small piece of black fondant and cut out two eyes to fit in the voids. It is a good idea to test that you have made the right shapes with pieces of tracing paper first, then press the black fondant into position. Break off pieces of the chocolate sticks and press them into the voids at the front and sides, using more apricot glaze to help them stay in place (Fig. 5).

5 Finally, stick the chocolate biscuits on to each side of the cake as earphones. To make them adhere use apricot glaze or a little icing sugar mixed to a sticky paste with some water.

SKELETOR

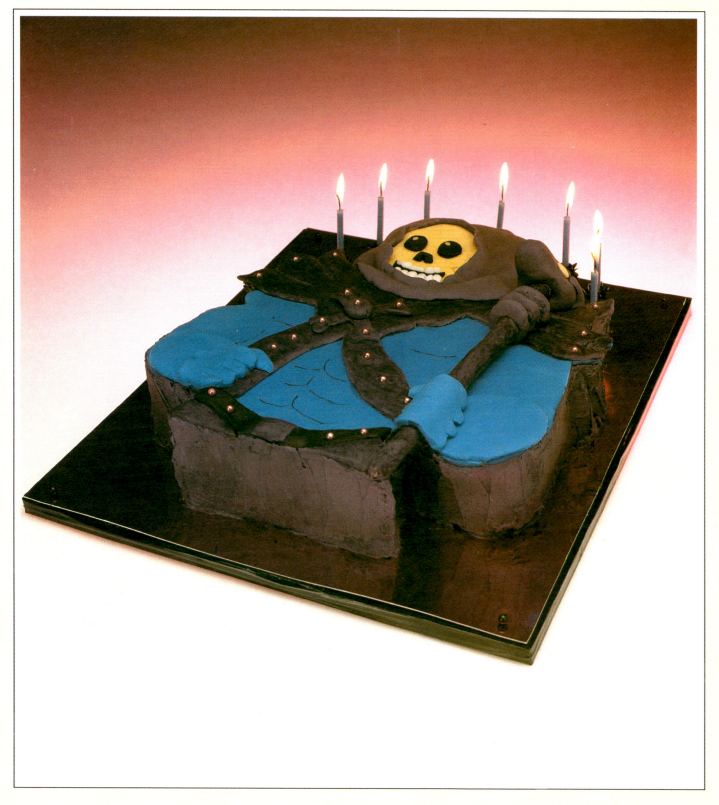

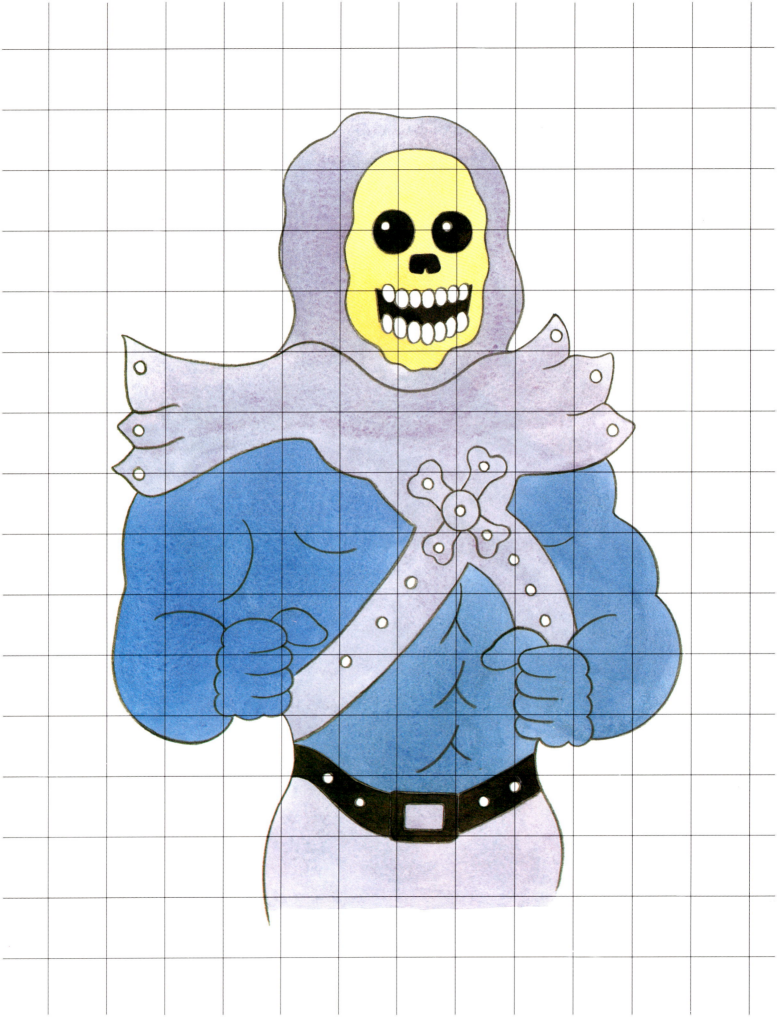

Skeletor is a villain from the comic *Masters of the Universe*. Perhaps the best way to beat him is to eat him.

You will need

1 12in × 10in (30cm × 25cm) cake
apricot glaze
1lb 5oz (600g) fondant: 8oz (225g) blue; 10oz (285g) mauve; 1oz (30g) pale yellow; 1oz (30g) black; pinch of white
candy stick
4oz (115g) butter icing
some coloured sugar balls
food-colouring pastes: mauve, yellow, and black

Method

1 Turn cake upside down on a board and, using your traced template, cut round Skeletor's complete face and body. Brush the top of the cake with apricot glaze.
2 Roll out the blue fondant and cut out a piece to cover the entire body from the neck downwards (Fig. 1). Keep any left-over blue fondant for lower arms and hands later.
3 Make a face from pale yellow fondant and place in position on the cake.
4 Roll out the mauve fondant. Using a separate traced drawing, cut out the cross piece of the tabard. Brush a little water on the blue body in roughly the position the tabard will sit and lift it gently into place (Fig. 2). Cut out an extra decorative piece for the centre, plus a small piece to fit around the waist. Gather up remaining fondant and knead again.
5 Cut out a separate tracing of the head and hood

and cut a hole in the centre where the face appears. Roll out the mauve fondant again and place this template in the centre. Leaving a border of about 2in (5cm) all round, cut out the hood piece. Lift it carefully over the yellow face and fold it over the edges of the cake. Cut off any unwanted surplus and save it for making the staff.
6 Roll out a piece of mauve fondant long enough and wide enough to cover your candy stick. Roll the fondant around the stick and pinch the edges together, wetting them if necessary. Make three smaller rolls of fondant and wrap each around the top of the stick, flattening the edges as you work. Mould another piece into the evil-looking head and add two small yellow eyes. Push the head on to the end of the stick and leave aside for the moment (Fig. 3).
7 Now for the rest of the arms and the hands. Roll out a small piece of blue fondant and cut out two extra lower arm pieces (see photograph). Stick in place with water. Cut out the hands. The Skeletor's right hand can be made in one piece and stuck in place. Make a tiny thumb for his left hand and stick down separately. Then place the staff on top of the body and wrap the hand piece over the top of it.
8 Using some black fondant, make a small belt, two eyes, a nose, and a mouth. Pinch off tiny pieces of white fondant to form some nasty-looking teeth and stick these around the mouth.
9 Colour the butter icing mauve and spread it around the sides of the cake with a palette knife.
10 Finally, decorate the tabard and belt with some coloured sugar balls.

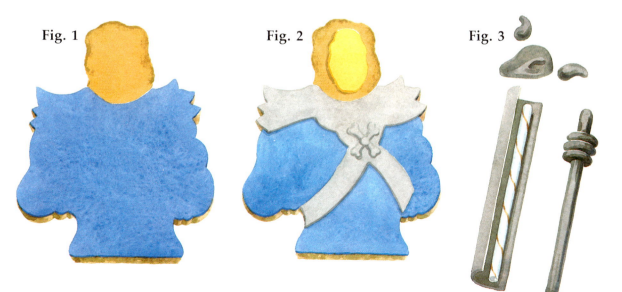

Fig. 1   Fig. 2   Fig. 3

THE SNOWMAN

This is Raymond Briggs's THE SNOWMAN™, who comes to life at Christmas and is befriended by a lonely little boy. A little bit of sculpting is called for, but you will quickly see the Snowman take shape as you layer up the cakes. You will need quite a lot of fondant to coat him completely, but it is well worth it. You could use royal icing instead, but the finish will then not be quite as smooth. I suggest that you use Madeira cake for the Snowman – sponge may be too soft to stand upright. You may like to split the two large cakes in half and sandwich the sections together with butter icing to make the cake even tastier.

You will need
1 8in (20cm) round cake
1 pudding-basin cake
2 4in (10cm) round cakes
12oz (340g) marzipan

apricot glaze
2lb 8oz (1.2kg) fondant: mainly white, but small quantities of green, black, and orange
8oz (225g) royal icing
food-colouring pastes: black, orange, green, and brown

Method
1 Place pudding-basin cake on top of the round cake and cut round the outside of the lower cake until the two cakes make a smooth outline together. If you like, just trim the lower cake slightly to narrow the base (Fig. 1).
2 Place the two small round cakes on the very top and cut and trim to fit together neatly (Fig. 1).
3 Dismantle the tower of cakes. Knead the marzipan until soft. Roll out a circle of marzipan slightly larger than the bottom of the cake. Round the edges with your fingertips to make little feet (Fig. 2).

Fig. 1

Fig. 2

Fig. 3

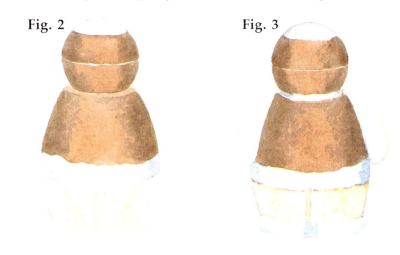

Fig. 4

Fig. 5

Fig. 6

4 Take another piece of marzipan and roll it into a circle about 1in (2.5cm) thick. Sandwich this between the round and the pudding-basin cakes. Push and mould the marzipan to make a smooth round 'tummy' (Fig. 2).

5 Round off the top and bottom of the two small head cakes with some marzipan to make a ball (Fig. 2).

6 Roll out two sausage-shaped pieces of marzipan for arms, and press them on to the sides of the body. With a sharp knife, make a V-shaped niche at the front of the body to suggest the outline of legs and feet (Fig. 3).

7 At this point you can remove the head – it will be covered in fondant separately.

8 Brush the body with apricot glaze.

9 Roll out the white fondant. You will have to judge how much you need to cover the whole of the Snowman's body, but it is better to roll out too much than too little.

10 Lift the rolled-out sheet of fondant with the aid of a rolling pin and position it over the Snowman's body, with the neck in the centre. Smooth the fondant down and round with the palms of your hands. Press it into the sides and cut off any surplus at the base with a sharp knife. You will also have to make snips and tucks where the fondant lies in a fold, but you can smooth out any cracks and rough joins later.

11 Next brush the head with apricot glaze, then knead and roll out the remaining white fondant. Cover the head in the same way as you did the body. Push head on to neck with a cocktail stick to secure it (Fig. 4).

12 Smooth round the Snowman with your fingertips, using a mixture of sifted icing sugar and cornflour to camouflage any cracks (Fig. 5).

13 Gather up remaining fondant and knead again. Pinch off a small piece and colour it black. Colour the rest green.

14 Roll out the green fondant and cut out a strip about 1in (2.5cm) wide to form a scarf. Snip the ends with scissors or a sharp knife to make a fringe, and wrap it round the Snowman's neck, sticking it down with water if necessary.

15 Fold the rest of the green fondant over the back of an upturned saucer and cut round the edge. Lift it from the saucer and press it down over the top of the Snowman's head. Lift up the edge to make a rim to the hat.

16 Make five small balls of black fondant for eyes and buttons, wet them and press them into the face and body. (Make dents in the white fondant with the back of a spoon handle to receive them.) Use a ball of orange-coloured fondant for the nose. Make a smiling mouth with a strip of black fondant or paint (Fig. 6).

17 Paint on stripes of orange and brown to make the hat and scarf look tweedy (Fig. 6).

18 Finally, spread some royal icing over the base and fork it through to look like snow.

FUNGUS THE BOGEYMAN

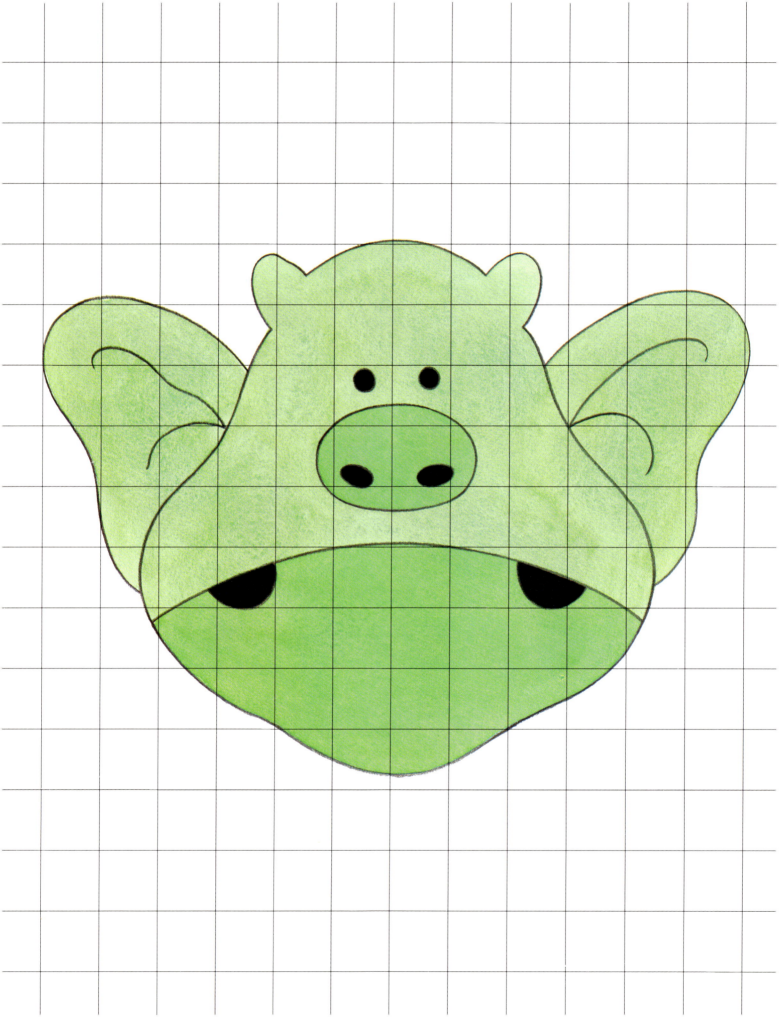

Invented, like the Snowman, by Raymond Briggs, Fungus doesn't like washing very much, has permanently smelly socks, and keeps a collection of pet snails and mice. He is a quick and easy cake to make.

You will need

1 12in × 10in (30cm × 25cm) cake
8oz (225g) marzipan
8oz (225g) butter icing
small quantity of peppermint essence (optional)
9oz (255g) fondant: 8oz (225g) green; pinch of black; pinch of grey
1 Swiss roll
apricot glaze
food-colouring pastes: green, orange, and black
a few strands of spaghetti

Method

1 Put a template of Fungus's head on the top of the cake and cut round it. There is no need to turn the cake upside down for this character.
2 Knead the marzipan until soft and roll out on a sugared board. Cut out a piece to fit over the upper part of the head and jaw, using a traced template. Place the marzipan on top of the cake as shown (Fig. 1).
3 Colour the butter icing green and, if you like, flavour it with a little peppermint essence. Spread it all over the sides and top of the cake, but do not cover the marzipan (Fig. 2).
4 Roll out green fondant and cut out shape of upper head and jaw to cover the marzipan. Press and shape over the edges of the marzipan to make sure it is well covered (Fig. 3).
5 Cut off a piece of Swiss roll, brush it with some apricot glaze, and cover this, too, in green fondant. Stick down with some water on top of the face (Fig. 3).

6 Finally, make two small eyes and two nostrils from black fondant and two large teeth from grey fondant. Paint some strands of spaghetti orange and push them into the top of Fungus's head.

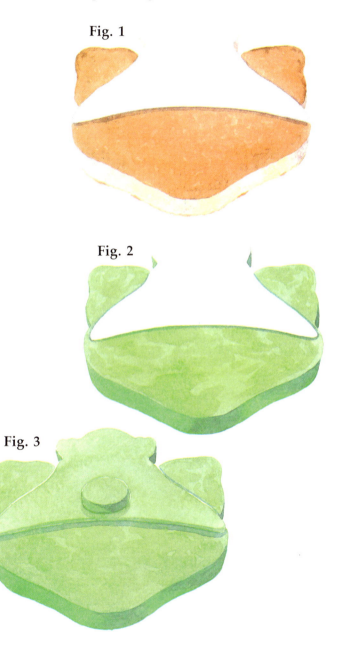

Fig. 1

Fig. 2

Fig. 3

MRS TIGGY-WINKLE

Here is Beatrix Potter's little domesticated hedgehog. You can see her take shape as you fit the cakes together, so don't be daunted. Take time to play around with marzipan when it comes to the sculpting stage – you will be surprised how easy it is to work with. This cake does take time to complete; it is not one to be rushed. I suggest that you use Madeira cake for the body – a sponge may be too soft.

You will need
1 pudding-basin cake
1 8in (20cm) round cake
2 4in (10cm) round cakes
4oz (115g) butter icing
1lb (450g) marzipan
apricot glaze
12oz (340g) ordinary fondant ⎫
12oz (340g) tragacanth fondant ⎭ mixed together
small packet of flaked almonds
food-colouring pastes: black, flesh, brown, and chestnut, plus colours of your choice for decorating the clothes

Method
1 Place the pudding-basin cake upside down on top of the 8in (20cm) round cake, overlapping it slightly at the back (Fig. 1).
2 Cut and trim the lower cake so that there is a small lip at the front – this will form the stomach. Make sure that the sides are level with the pudding-basin cake (Fig. 2).
3 With a sharp knife, shave the sides of the lower cake slightly inwards towards the base (Fig. 3, front view). Continue to shave the top cake so that a gentle slope is formed at the front. This is where the head will sit. Cut away a small piece of cake from the back to accentuate the shape of the bustle (Fig. 4, side view).
4 At this stage you can sandwich the two cakes together with butter icing.
5 Rest the two 4in (10cm) round cakes together on top of the body, using a toothpick as a temporary support if necessary. You will probably need to level off the bottom of both so that they sit comfortably in position. Carve and shave them until they become

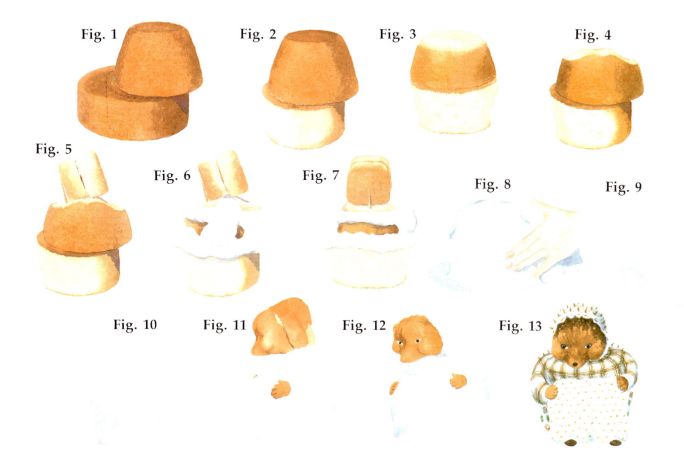

Fig. 1   Fig. 2   Fig. 3   Fig. 4

Fig. 5   Fig. 6   Fig. 7   Fig. 8   Fig. 9

Fig. 10   Fig. 11   Fig. 12   Fig. 13

smoother and rounder (Fig. 5). Leave them in position while you build up the body with marzipan, because they will make it easier to see Mrs Tiggy-winkle's shape as the cake forms.

6 Brush the two body cakes with apricot glaze. Knead the marzipan until soft. Shape small pieces into rolls and press them on to the sides and front of the body to round off the bustle and stomach and to form a bustline (Fig. 6).

7 Mould two pieces of marzipan into small round arms and press these too on to the sides (Fig. 7). Keep moulding the marzipan with your fingertips until you are fairly happy with the overall shape. When fondant is applied any flaws will be camouflaged.

8 Remove the two head cakes and brush another layer of apricot glaze over the entire cake. Take the fondant out of its bag and knead it again thoroughly on a floured and sugared board. Roll it out until it is large enough to cover the cake. Carefully lift up the fondant with the aid of a rolling pin and fold it over the body. Working quickly, cut off the surplus, otherwise it may pull little tears and cracks and spoil the final finish. Smooth the fondant down into the shapes formed by the marzipan with the palms of your hands (Fig. 8).

9 The main body will now begin to take on a familiar appearance (Figs. 9 and 10). Make two little balls of fondant into feet and stick them on to the board with apricot glaze. Gather up any spare fondant, knead it again, and roll it thinly. Cut out a small square to make an apron. Brush the front of the stomach with a little water and press the apron in place around the waist, pinching the top into pleats and letting the bottom fall and fold over the shoes (Fig. 11).

10 Take about 6oz (170g) of remaining marzipan, knead it, and colour it to imitate flesh. First make the face. Mould marzipan over the front of one of the 4in (10cm) round cakes to make small round cheeks and a long pointy nose. Stick the second cake on the back and add more marzipan, moulding it into a bonnet shape. Then stick the head on top of the body with apricot glaze or butter icing. Make two little hands from flesh-coloured marzipan and stick them on to the body on top of the apron (Fig. 11).

11 Using the end of a teaspoon handle press two tiny ears into the face. Brush the back of the head with apricot glaze and roll out a small piece of fondant into a circle. Press this in place to make a mob cap. Pinch little pleats at the front into a frill. Dig two tiny holes in the face for eyes and fill them with small pieces of fondant. Paint on the irises in brown (Fig. 12).

12 Toast the almonds gently under a medium grill and then push them carefully into the head and back to form spines. Paint their ends brown if you wish. Paint Mrs Tiggy-winkle's face with streaks of pale chestnut brown and the hair on her head and hands with a darker brown. Don't forget to give her a brown nose (Fig. 13).

13 Finally paint in her clothes. Beatrix Potter's Mrs Tiggy-winkle has a spotless white apron and cap, but I have added splashes of yellow for extra colour. I used pink and green for her flowery overdress and skirt, but, if you wish, keep to the colours used in the original illustrations – pinks, blue, and grey.

WINNIE-THE-POOH

Here is Pooh, the bear with a passion for honey, sitting on a grassy bank, probably deciding what to have for lunch. He is quite simple to make, with minimum cutting of cake and fondant.

You will need

1 12in × 10in (30cm × 25cm) cake
6oz (170g) butter icing
apricot glaze
11oz (310g) fondant: 6oz (170g) yellow; 4oz (115g) red; pinch of black
3oz (85g) desiccated coconut
food-colouring pastes: yellow, red, green, and black

Method

1 Turn the cake upside down. Cut out Pooh's outline from a traced template and place on top of cake. Cut round it and include the piece that will form the grassy bank at the bottom. Cut out an extra arm and leg from the offcuts of cake as indicated in the template.

2 Take about 3tbs (45ml) of butter icing and colour it green. Put aside. Colour the rest yellow and spread over the sides of the cake that will form Pooh's body.

3 Brush top of cake with apricot glaze. Roll out yellow fondant and cut out Pooh's body, using a tracing. Place over top of cake (Fig. 1). Gather up surplus trimmings and knead again. Make sure extra arm and leg pieces of cake are trimmed and smooth and apply apricot glaze. Then cover them in yellow fondant. Put aside until required (Fig. 2).

4 Roll out red fondant and cut out a little shirt piece. Stick down on top of the yellow fondant body. Leave extra pieces of red fondant at the ends to cover the sides of the cake if you wish (Fig. 3).

5 Cover the top of the extra arm cake with a piece of red fondant to look like a sleeve (Fig. 2). Place the arm and leg on the cake (Fig. 4).

6 Spread the green butter icing that you put aside over the remaining part of the cake. Colour the coconut green and sprinkle it liberally over the icing to make a grassy bank.

7 Finally, make a small blob of black fondant into a nose, and eye, and an eyebrow. Paint on Pooh's smiling mouth with a paintbrush, and your happy little bear is complete.

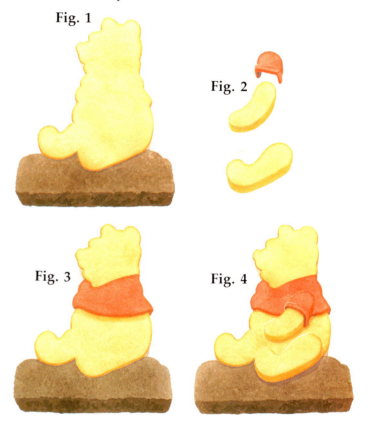

Fig. 1

Fig. 2

Fig. 3

Fig. 4

THOMAS THE TANK ENGINE

This cake looks more complicated than it really is – it is made entirely from a Swiss roll and a 12in × 10in (30cm × 25cm) cake. Follow the instructions step by step, and if one of your cake pieces does not fit simply cut or shave it until it does. The fun is in adding the final touches – the wheels, chimneys, and bumpers.

You will need
1 12in × 10in (30cm × 25cm) cake
1 Swiss roll
8oz (225g) marzipan

apricot glaze
8oz (225g) butter icing
14oz (400g) fondant: 2oz (60g) white; 3oz (85g) red; 4oz (115g) black; 3oz (85g) blue; 2oz (60g) yellow
round biscuit
6 liquorice Catherine wheels
liquorice allsorts
food-colouring pastes: blue, black, red, and yellow

Method
1 Cut the Swiss roll to make it about 5½in (14cm) long. Cut another slice from the remainder and slice it in half to make two half circles. Put these aside (Fig. 1).

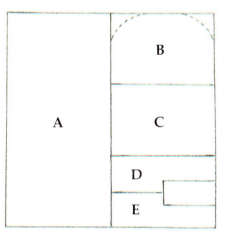

Fig. 1

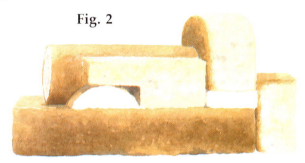

Fig. 2

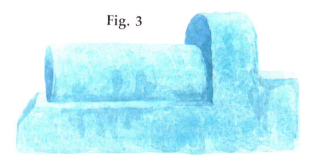

Fig. 3

Fig. 4

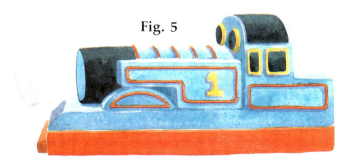

Fig. 5

Fig. 6

2 Flatten the top of the cake if necessary and turn it upside down. Divide it up as shown in Fig. 1.

3 Place the base, A, on your board and fill any gaps with pieces of softened marzipan. Place the Swiss roll on the top.

4 Trim B as shown in Fig. 1, to make a rounded top, and place it behind the Swiss roll on top of piece A. You will probably need a small piece of marzipan about ½in (1.25cm) thick stuck beneath it for a little extra height. Trim and square up piece C and place it at the back (Fig. 2).

5 Cut the final section of the cake to make pieces D and E. They may be too thick to fit neatly at the sides of the engine so, again, cut and trim to a suitable size. Place them on base A beside the Swiss roll, together with the half circles (Fig. 2).

6 Use some apricot glaze to stick all the pieces together.

7 Cut off the corner piece of base A to make a neat profile (Fig. 3).

8 Colour about 2tbs (30ml) butter icing red, and the rest blue. At this stage you can cover the entire cake with blue butter icing if you wish (Fig. 3). I decided to cover the side pieces D and E and the Swiss roll halves in blue fondant to give a variety of textures, but the choice is yours (Fig. 4). Spread the butter icing carefully with a small palette knife dipped in warm water to give as smooth a finish as possible. If you have covered the side pieces of cake with fondant, push them back on to the main cake now with the help of some apricot glaze to make them stick.

9 Roll out the yellow fondant and cut out two 1in (2.5cm) squares and two 1in × ½in (2.5cm × 1.25cm) rectangles for the side windows and four small circles for the front and back windows. Also cut out the two numerals for the sides of the engine. Put these pieces aside for the moment.

10 Roll out the black fondant and cut out one 2in × 4½in (5cm × 11.5cm) rectangle for the roof and one 1½in × 4in (4cm × 10cm) rectangle for the engine. Also cut out pieces slightly smaller than the yellow window pieces and stick them over the yellow pieces. Stick the larger black fondant pieces in position at the front of the engine and over the roof, then position the windows and the numerals (Fig. 5).

11 Roll out the red fondant and cut out two 10in × 1in (25cm × 2.5cm) strips for the sides of the train and two 4½in × 1in (11.5cm × 2.5cm) strips for the back and front. Push gently into position at the base of the cake (Fig. 5).

12 Roll out the remaining white fondant and, using your biscuit as a template, cut out a circle. Press this over the biscuit and smooth over the edges. With your fingers pinch three more pieces of white fondant into shapes to make small cheeks and a nose. Press and mould these on to the front of the face. Using a small paintbrush dipped in black paste, paint on eyes, eyebrows, and a mouth. Stick the face on to front of the engine using butter icing (Fig. 5).

13 Fill a piping bag with red butter icing and carefully pipe small thin lines round the top of the engine and on the side pieces. (See Fig. 5 and photograph.)

14 Stick liquorice allsorts together with icing to make one black and one blue chimney. Stick these on the cake. Press three liquorice Catherine wheels on each side of the cake and two black liquorice allsorts into the front as bumpers (Fig. 6).

15 Finally make some small nuggets of coal from black fondant and pile them on to the back of the engine.

MR MEN

Simple and colourful, these biscuits represent five of the many kinds of Mr Men. Make any of the other characters not included here by drawing your own templates.

You will need, to make 24 biscuits
8oz (225g) plain flour
pinch of salt
½tsp (2.5ml) baking powder
4oz (115g) butter
6oz (170g) caster sugar
1 egg
1tsp (5ml) vanilla essence
1lb (450g) royal icing
food-colouring pastes: blue, red, green, yellow, pink, and black.

Method
1 Sift together flour, salt, and baking powder. Cream the butter and sugar, add the egg and vanilla essence, and beat well. Add the sifted flour etc., a little at a time, and mix until well blended. Wrap and chill this dough in the refrigerator for at least 40mins before rolling it.

2 Meanwhile, cut out the Mr Men templates. Trace the shapes on to thin cardboard if you can, because each will be used several times and greaseproof paper will not last as long.

3 Preheat oven to 200°C (400°F), Gas mark 6. Roll out a third of the dough at a time and carefully cut out the Mr Men from the templates. Place on greased baking sheets and bake in the oven for 10mins. Cool on wire racks.

4 Divide the royal icing between five small bowls and colour each one differently. Spread the icing over the biscuits with a teaspoon, spreading it to the edges with a cocktail stick.

5 When the icing has hardened, paint on the eyes and mouths with a small paintbrush and some black food colouring. Mr Worry's nose is a glacé cherry.

NODDY AND HIS CAR

Noddy's car is his most prized possession, and here it is in all its glory. The car will take shape very quickly as soon as you cut up the two cakes as shown and place them on top of one another. Patience is needed, though, for the finer details of the lights and bumpers and for moulding Noddy out of marzipan.

You will need

1 12in × 10in (30cm × 25cm) cake
1 9in (22.5cm) square cake
1 chocolate Swiss roll
apricot glaze
3lb (1.4kg) fondant: 1lb 6oz (625g) yellow; 10oz (285g) red; 6oz (170g) blue; 5oz (140g) pink; 5oz (140g) grey
icing sugar
8oz (225g) marzipan
liquorice Catherine wheel
8oz (225g) royal icing or butter icing (optional)
non-toxic silver paint (optional)
3oz (85g) desiccated coconut (optional)
food-colouring pastes: yellow, red, blue, flesh, pink, black, brown, and green

Method

1 Cut both the cakes into three large sections, A, B, and C, as indicated in Fig. 1. Cut two smaller pieces, D and E, from the 9in (22.5cm) cake for doors and save piece F, which you will need later to make the car seat. There will be a long piece of the large cake left over.

2 Turn piece A upside down on your board and place B and C on top (Fig. 2). Stick the pieces together with some apricot glaze. Trim D and E to make sure they fit in the gaps (Fig. 3) and then remove them to be used later.

3 Cut off the sides of the cake at the front to form the bonnet (Fig. 4). Then, with a sharp knife, shave and round off the corners of the top of the cake (Fig. 5).

4 Carve out an L-shaped seat from F and place it in position between pieces D and E to make sure it fits snugly (Fig. 6). Carve a slight U shape at the top of D and E so that they look more like doors. Then remove all three pieces until ready to be covered in fondant.

Fig. 1   Fig. 2   Fig. 3
Fig. 4   Fig. 5   Fig. 6
Fig. 7   Fig. 8   Fig. 9
Fig. 10   Fig. 11   Fig. 12

71

5 Spread some apricot glaze over the front and back sections of the car. Roll out the yellow fondant and cover each section separately (Fig. 7). Knead surplus fondant again and keep nearby.

6 Roll out the pink fondant. Cut a piece to fit over the floor of the car. Cover the seat with apricot glaze followed by pink fondant and place in position. Make tiny dents on the back of the seat with a teaspoon handle (Fig. 8).

7 Take pieces D and E and stick them at the ends of the seat with more glaze. Roll out two more sections of yellow fondant and cover the remaining exposed cake to form the doors (Fig. 9).

8 Cut the Swiss roll into five pieces for the wheels (including a spare wheel for the back of the car). Roll out some more yellow fondant and cut out five small circles for the hub caps. Stick them over the sides of the Swiss roll with a little glaze. Then stick the wheels on to the sides of the car with some paste made from a mixture of icing sugar and water (Fig. 10).

9 Knead the red fondant until soft and form it into four chunky mudguards – one for each wheel (Fig. 11).

10 Now for the details. Use the grey fondant to mould two small door handles, four headlamps and two rear-lights. Roll out a large flat piece for the front grill and two long sausages for the front and back bumpers. Stick all the pieces in place by brushing a drop or two of water on the car to make sure they stick fast (Figs. 12, 13 and 14).

11 To make the hood of the car, roll out the blue fondant into a large thin piece. Then pleat it over itself to suggest a folded-down hood (Fig. 15). Cut out the shape of the hood with a knife and place it in position at the back of the car.

12 The penultimate step is to mould a marzipan Noddy. Colour about 6oz (170g) of marzipan red for his body and the remainder flesh for his head. Shape the body to form two arms and stick two small pieces of flesh marzipan on the ends as hands. Make a tiny

Fig. 13

Fig. 14

Fig. 15

Fig. 16

pinch of flesh-coloured marzipan into a nose and press it on to the face. Form the eyes from two pieces of white fondant and push them into place. Paint on the blue bits of the eyes, a red mouth, and the eyebrows (Fig. 16). Now sit Noddy in the driver's seat and cut off a piece of liquorice to fit between his hands as a steering wheel. It may be tricky at first to make all the pieces of marzipan stick together, but persevere and continue moulding them until you are satisfied with the finished appearance. Roll out a piece of yellow fondant to make Noddy's scarf and a piece of blue fondant for his hood. Cut the blue fondant into a triangular shape and wrap it round his head. Use a blob of yellow fondant for a bell at the end. Noddy's scarf should of course have red dots on it, so please add these if you wish to be really accurate. Either use a tiny piece of brown-coloured fondant for his hair or colour a spoonful of royal icing brown and gently fork it over the edge of the hood. Make two tiny ears from flesh marzipan and stick in place over the hood as well.

13 To finish off the car you can either paint the front grill directly on to the grey fondant in black or you can paint all the pieces of grey fondant with non-toxic silver first. Just bear in mind that these pieces must be removed before the cake is eaten as no one has yet invented a silver colour that is edible.

14 Complete the base by spreading some green-coloured royal icing or butter icing over the board and liberally sprinkling it with green-coloured coconut.

THE OWL AND THE PUSSY-CAT

The Owl and the Pussy-cat went to sea
In a beautiful pea-green boat,
They took some honey, and plenty of money,
Wrapped up in a five-pound note.

Here is Edward Lear's poem in edible form. The little marzipan animals are not difficult to make – they are constructed basically from two balls of marzipan, one for the head and one for the body.

You will need
1 9in (22.5cm) square cake
apricot glaze
1lb 8oz (680g) fondant
4oz (115g) butter icing
8oz (225g) royal icing
8oz (225g) marzipan
packet small round mints
food-colouring pastes: green, pink, blue, brown and
    yellow
sheet of rice paper
wooden stick

Method
1 Cut the cake as shown in Fig. 1. Use piece A for the main body of the boat. Place it flat side down on your board and level the top. Place pieces B and C on top, curved sides uppermost, and trim off the ends (Fig. 2).
2 Remove B and C and brush all three pieces with apricot glaze.
3 Colour the fondant green and roll out. Cover A, B, and C with fondant, cutting off the surplus as necessary. Replace B and C in their original positions.
4 Colour the butter icing pink and pipe thin lines around the boat, using a no.1 or 2 nozzle.
5 Colour the royal icing blue and spread over the board. Swirl it round in circles with a spoon to look like waves.
6 Colour half of the marzipan brown for the owl and leave the rest white for the cat. Make their heads and bodies from small balls (Fig. 3). Mould two wings for the owl and two little arms for the cat and make their legs and feet in separate pieces. You can give them hats to wear if you wish. Paint on the cat's eyes, nose, and whiskers in brown. Push small circles of white marzipan into the owl's head for eyes and mould and paint a small beak yellow. Push all the pieces of their bodies together and sit them gently in the boat.
7 Decorate the boat with mints as shown.
8 Paint a short wooden stick red using non-toxic paint or food colour. Stick on a rice-paper sail with some royal icing and push into the centre of the boat.

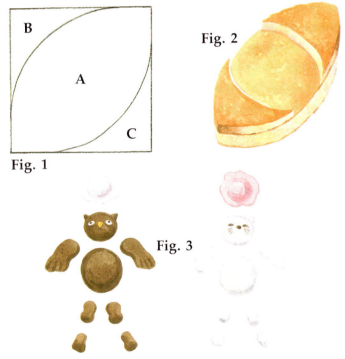

Fig. 1

Fig. 2

Fig. 3

THE PIG WITH A RING

And there in a wood a Piggy-wig stood
With a ring at the end of his nose,
His nose,
His nose,
With a ring at the end of his nose.

This is the character from Edward Lear's 'The Owl and the Pussy-cat' who sold his ring to the happy couple. This is a fairly substantial cake that will feed twenty-five to thirty people. As quite a lot of fondant and marzipan is required, do make sure that it is all properly softened and kneaded together. Work quickly once the paste has been coated over the cakes, cutting and trimming the surplus to prevent tears appearing. Don't forget to remove the ring before eating – gold paint is not edible. You can also split all three cakes in two and sandwich the pieces together with butter icing for an extra treat.

You will need
3 pudding-basin cakes
1 Swiss roll
apricot glaze
12oz (340g) marzipan
1lb 4oz (570g) fondant ⎫ kneaded together
1lb 4oz (570g) marzipan ⎭ and flesh coloured
icing sugar
stick of candy or toothpicks (optional)
food-colouring pastes: flesh, gold, blue, and black

Method
1 Level off bases of cakes if necessary and stack on top of each other as shown in Fig. 1. You can stick them all together with either apricot glaze or some butter icing.
2 Round off the top cake by shaving it with a sharp knife to smooth off the edges. Knead about 12oz (340g) of marzipan until soft and break into pieces. Mould and shape to form cheeks and a little chin and press on to the sides of the cake as shown (Fig. 2). Brush all over the cake with apricot glaze.
3 Roll out the fondant/marzipan mix (this mixture gives a lovely soft skin texture). It can be quite thick as it will then be much easier to handle. Carefully lift it up on a rolling pin and place it centrally over the top of the cakes. Press the fondant over the sides of the cakes with your fingertips and cut off the excess (Fig. 3). You will have to trim off quite a lot, so gather

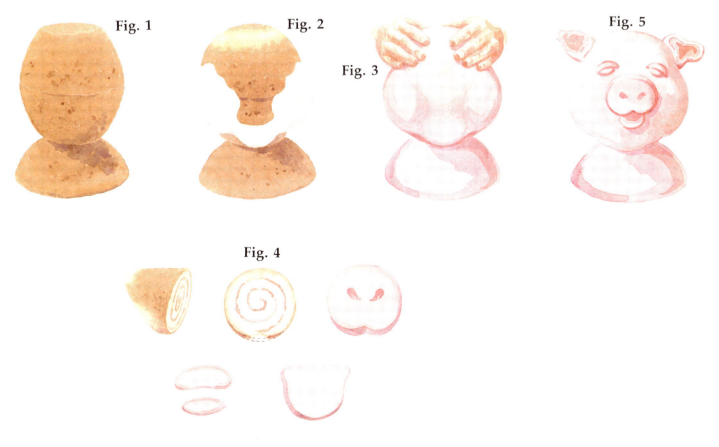

Fig. 1

Fig. 2

Fig. 3

Fig. 5

Fig. 4

up any surplus and knead again. It will be used for the ears, nose, eyes and mouth.

4 Cut off a section of Swiss roll (Fig. 4). Cut a small niche at the base as shown. Spread some apricot glaze on the front and sides and cover in fondant/marzipan mixture. Make nostril indentations with a teaspoon handle. Stick the nose on the face with the aid of a little paste made from icing sugar and water. You may find this a little tricky so try using a stick of candy or a couple of toothpicks to join the nose to the face. Make the eyes from two oval pieces pushed together (Fig. 4) and make a small round piece for the mouth. These will stick on the face quite easily with a little brushed-on water. Similarly, mould two round, floppy ears and press in place (Fig. 5.).

5 Leave the pig to dry out for a few hours before painting the eyes with blue colouring. Add a tiny iris made from black fondant.

6 Roll out a tiny sausage of fondant/marzipan and press the ends into the nostrils. Again, wait until it has dried out and then paint it with gold food paint to look like a ring. (Don't forget that gold paint is not edible – remove the ring before eating.)

7 Finally, colour some icing sugar with a dash of pink and dab on to the cheeks and inner ears for a rosy glow.

HANSEL AND GRETEL

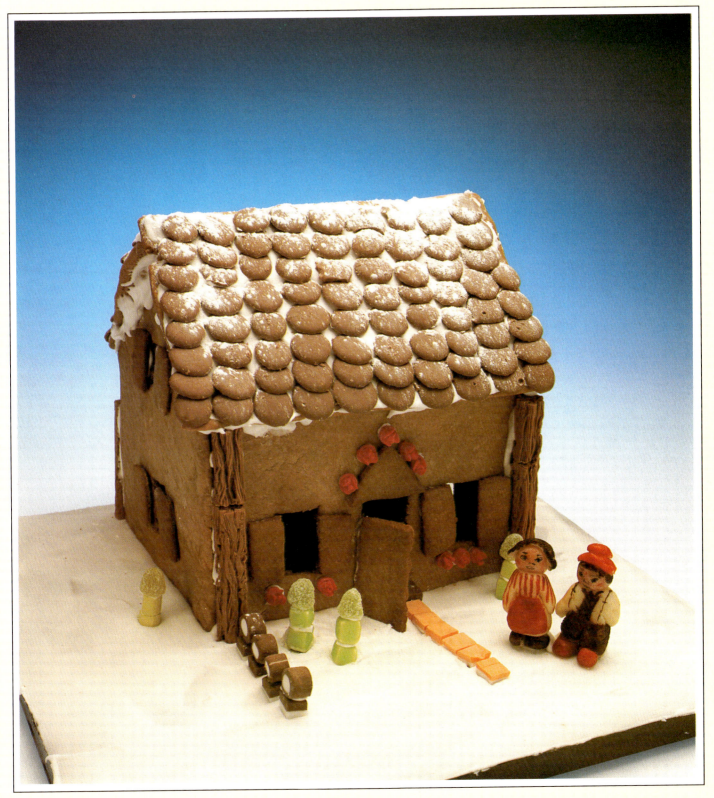

The house, from the fairy tale by the brothers Grimm, can be any size and shape you like and can be decorated with sweets and chocolates to your own taste. Use the instructions as a guide, but by all means adapt them.

You will need, for the house
9oz (255g) plain flour
1tsp (5ml) ground ginger
1tsp (5ml) bicarbonate of soda
3oz (85g) margarine
4½oz (130g) soft brown sugar
2tbs (30ml) golden syrup
1 egg
royal icing

Method

1 Sift flour, ginger, and bicarbonate of soda into a bowl. Rub in the margarine with your fingertips until the mixture resembles fine breadcrumbs. Stir in the sugar, add the syrup and beaten egg, and mix together into a pliable dough. Roll into a ball, wrap in cling film, and chill for at least two hours.

2 Meanwhile, cut the templates for the house out of two or three sheets of greaseproof paper. The sizes I have suggested are for guidance only; adapt them and make a house of any design you like.

3 Grease two large baking sheets and cut the dough in two pieces before rolling out. Roll out the dough on a floured board and cut out the six pieces from your templates. Lift them onto the baking sheet with the aid of a spatula. Do not cut out the windows and door until the dough is on the baking sheets as the shape will spoil if you try to lift it. Gather up remaining dough and cut out the shutters (Fig. 1).

4 Bake in a preheated oven at 190°C (375°F), Gas mark 5, for 15 mins – until the gingerbread is golden brown. Leave on the baking sheet until the pieces firm up, then cool on a wire rack.

5 Stick the little shutters at the sides of the windows with some royal icing and leave to dry.

Fig. 1

Fig. 2

You will need, for the figures and decorations
1lb (450g) royal icing
4 chocolate flakes
2 packets chocolate buttons
4oz (115g) marzipan
icing sugar
assorted food-colouring pastes and coloured sweets

Method
1 Spread royal icing all over your board. While still wet, assemble all the pieces of the gingerbread house together and glue them to each other with royal icing. Start with the sides of the house and wait for the icing to dry out a little before adding the roof pieces. Add the door at the front and leave it slightly open. Add a chocolate flake to each corner. Spread more icing over the roof as a base for the chocolate buttons. Layer them up in rows to look like tiles.

2 Dust some sifted icing sugar over them to look like freshly fallen snow. Mould two tiny figures from marzipan to form Hansel and Gretel (Fig. 2). When they have dried out, paint on their faces and clothes with food paint. Place them in the snow outside the house.

3 Finish by decorating the house with any little sweets you choose.

HUMPTY DUMPTY

This cake depicts poor Humpty Dumpty before his fall. It is a large cake that will feed at least thirty hungry children.

You will need, for the wall
1 12in × 10in (30cm × 25cm) cake
1lb (450g) butter icing
packet chocolate mint thins

Method
1 Cut the cake in half across its width and place the two pieces on top of one another.
2 Cover the cakes with butter icing, making the surface as smooth as you can.
3 Press the chocolate thins on to the sides (not the top) of the wall, to look like bricks.

You will need, for Humpty Dumpty
2 pudding-basin cakes
12oz (340g) marzipan
apricot glaze
2lb 8oz (1.1kg) fondant: 1lb 8oz (680g) flesh and caramel colours mixed (to get the egg's colour); 8oz (225g) blue; 6oz (170g) white; pinch each of black and red
food-colouring pastes: flesh, caramel, blue, red and black
cocktail stick (optional)

Method
1 Level tops of the cakes and place them one above the other. Fill any gaps in the centre with softened pieces of marzipan and also add a section of marzipan

Fig. 1

Fig. 2

Fig. 3

Fig. 4

Fig. 5

83

at the top to complete the egg shape. Shave round the centre with a sharp knife to make the cakes as smooth and round as you can (Fig. 1). Brush all over with apricot glaze.

2 Roll out the flesh/caramel fondant into a piece that you estimate will cover the whole egg. Lift it carefully onto the top of the egg, using a rolling pin to help you. Quickly smooth down the fondant with your fingertips and cut off any surplus. Keep this in a polythene bag until you need it again (Fig. 2).

3 Now place egg carefully on the wall.

4 Roll out a piece of blue fondant to cover the lower third of the egg. (You may like to check the exact length of fondant you need by measuring around the base of the egg with a tape measure.) Brush the base with a little water first and then press the blue fondant into position (Fig. 3).

5 Cut out a small circle of white fondant and a smaller circle of black for each eye and stick on to the egg. With the surplus flesh/caramel fondant make a nose, mouth, and eye lids and stick these, too, on to the egg (Fig. 4). You may need a cocktail stick to keep the nose in place. Paint the whites of the eyes blue.

6 Roll out the white fondant and cut a small triangular-shaped piece for the front of Humpty's shirt. Add a tiny red fondant tie. Cut a long strip of white fondant about 1in (2.5cm) wide for the shirt collar and wrap around the top of the blue shirt, sticking it in place with a little water. Fold down the corners to complete (Fig. 5).

7 At this stage you can complete the wall by filling in the top with chocolate pieces.

8 Make small arms and legs from sausages of blue fondant and stick them to the sides of the egg cake. Hang the legs over the wall and add white cuffs to the ends of the arms.

8 Finally, make hands from egg-coloured fondant and boots from black fondant. And there is your Humpty Dumpty. Eat him before he falls!

DALEK

This is one of the extra-terrestrial 'exterminators' from the television series *Dr Who*. Daleks are actually made from metal, but this one is made from chocolate because it tastes better.

You will need
1 jug or flower-pot cake*
1 4in (10cm) round cake
8oz (225g) chocolate butter icing
3oz (85g) fondant
apricot glaze
2 round biscuits
chocolate biscuit
box chocolate mint thins
packet Maltesers
chocolate finger
chocolate sticks
food-colouring paste: brown

* I bake this cake in a well-greased 2-litre stainless-steel jug. If you have no metal jug that will withstand an hour or so in the oven, I find it just as easy to use an earthenware flower pot. Make sure it is clean, grease it as you would a cake tin, and it will make a perfect Dalek-shaped cake. For either receptacle use a Madeira mix of: 10oz (285g) butter; 10oz (285g) caster sugar; 10oz (285g) self-raising flour; 5oz (140g) plain flour; 5 eggs.

Method
1 Cover the main cake with chocolate butter icing, and make it as smooth as you can with a palette knife dipped in hot water.
2 Shave the sides of the small cake until it forms a smooth hemisphere. Then cover it in fondant, coloured either with brown food colouring or a mixture of cocoa powder and artificial chocolate flavouring.

Brush on some apricot glaze first to help the fondant stick.
3 Layer up the round biscuits, chocolate biscuit, and small cake as shown in Fig. 1, using a dash of butter icing to stick them all in place.
4 Break up a few chocolate mint thins into small oblong pieces and push them into the top of the main body of the Dalek.
5 Push rows of Maltesers into the rest of the cake, and a couple into the head for eyes. If the Maltesers slip off, cut them in half and you will find they stay put.
6 Use a chocolate finger for the Dalek's antenna and chocolate sticks for the blast guns. Make a small ball of white fondant and three balls of brown fondant and push them on to the ends of the sticks.
7 Cut a strip of brown fondant to tidy the base if you wish.

Fig. 1

GROUCHO MARX

Here is perhaps the best-loved Marx brother, complete with characteristic moustache, distinctive nose, glasses, and cigar. He is very easy to make and can be completed within an hour.

You will need

1 12in × 10in (30cm × 25cm) cake
apricot glaze
14oz (400g) fondant: 9oz (255g) flesh colour; 5oz (140g) black
1lb (450g) royal icing
some liquorice strands
2 chocolate fingers
food-colouring pastes: flesh and black

Method

1 Pin the template of Groucho's face to the top of the cake and cut it to shape. Cover with a coating of apricot glaze. Cut out another template of the face, this time without the hair. Roll out the flesh-coloured fondant and place the template in the centre. Cut round the top of the forehead but leave a border of about 2in (5cm) around the remainder of the template to provide for covering the sides of the cake. Lift the fondant carefully on to the cake, easing it over the sides and smoothing it down with your fingertips. Cut off excess (Fig. 1).

2 Gather up surplus flesh fondant and knead again. Mould two eyes, two ears, the lower half of the mouth, and a large nose. Stick these to the face with a little water. Similarly, make two eyebrows and a moustache with black fondant (Fig. 2).

3 Colour the royal icing black and spread it over the hair area and also over the pieces of black fondant. Use a fork to carefully peak it into curls while it is still wet.

4 Unravel some strands of liquorice and form them into a pair of glasses. Rest them over the eyes and eyebrows and around the tops of the ears.

5 Groucho would not be complete without a cigar, so take two chocolate fingers and gently push them into his mouth for the finishing touch.

Fig. 1

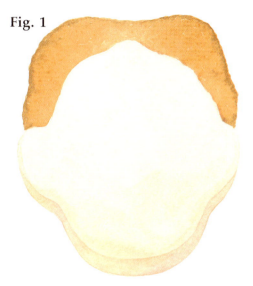

Fig. 2

BIRTHDAY CARE BEAR

Care Bears have become very popular with younger children and a Care Bear cake will delight them on any occasion. Adapt the instructions to make any of the other Care Bears by making different designs on the tummy in fondant and colouring each bear according to its character – blue for Grumpy, green for Good Luck Bear, and pink for Cheer Bear.

You will need

1 12in × 10in (30cm × 25cm) cake
8oz (225g) marzipan
apricot glaze
12oz (340g) fondant: 8oz (225g) orange-brown; 3oz (85g) white; pinches of pink, blue, yellow, red, and black
6oz (170g) butter icing
food-colouring pastes: caramel, brown, orange, pink, blue, yellow, red and black

Method

1 Level off cake and turn it upside down. Cut round the Birthday Bear's outline from a traced template (Figs. 1 and 2).

2 Knead the marzipan until soft. Pinch off two small pieces and roll them in the palms of your hands to make smooth, rounded cheeks. Place them on the Bear's face. Using the rest of the marzipan, make his tummy a little fatter and rounder as shown (Fig. 3). Brush over the cake with apricot glaze.

3 Roll out the brown fondant. (I used three colours – caramel, brown, and orange mixed together – to make a good colour.) Using your original Care Bear template cut out another shape in fondant. Lift it very carefully on to the cake, easing it into position over the marzipan (Fig. 4). Make two extra round ear pieces and stick these in position with a little water.

Fig. 1

Fig. 2

Fig. 3

Fig. 4

Fig. 5

4 Pinch off a piece of white fondant and roll it into a ball to make a nose. Shape it as in the drawing. Stick it on to the face between the two cheeks. Make a mouth and two eyes.

5 Roll out the remaining white fondant and cut out a circular piece to cover the tummy, using a tracing. Try and cut out a shape slightly larger than the tracing to allow for the enlarged shape of the marzipan underneath.

6 Roll out a pinch each of pink, blue, and yellow fondant and cut out shapes to make the cake motif. Stick in position on the white fondant. Make a tiny heart to stick on the nose (Fig. 5).

7 Colour the butter icing to match the body colour as closely as you can and spread it carefully over the sides of the cake.

8 Finally, when the fondant has dried out a little, paint on tiny eyebrows and eye pupils in black.

USEFUL ADDRESSES

The following are suppliers of all equipment essential to the cake maker including food colours. They will also provide a mail-order service.

Covent Garden Kitchen Supplies
Unit 2
The Market
Covent Garden
London WC2
Tel (01) 836 9167

Elizabeth David Ltd
46 Bourne Street
London SW1
Tel (01) 730 3123

Mary Ford Cake Artistry Centre Ltd
28 Southbourne Grove
Southbourne
Bournemouth
BH6 3RA
Tel 0202 422653

David Mellor
26 James Street
London WC2
Tel (01) 379 6947
&
4 Sloane Square
London SW1
Tel (01) 730 4259

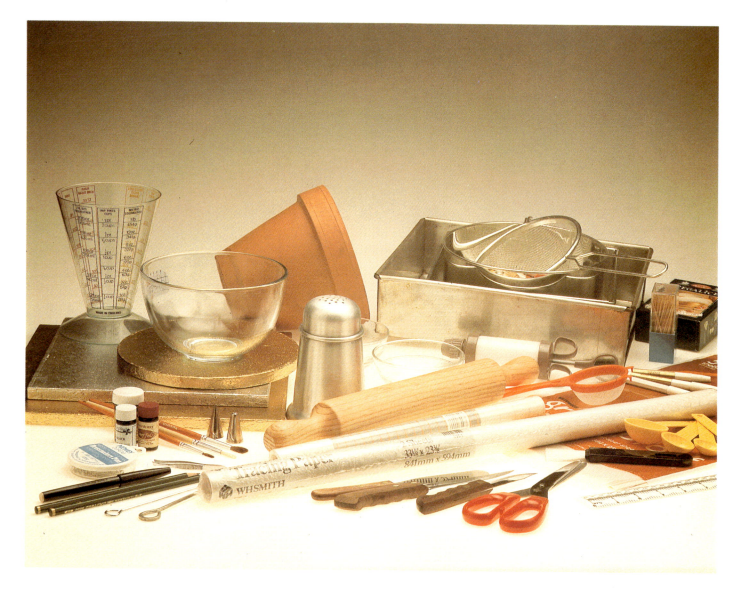

ACKNOWLEDGEMENTS

My thanks to Amy Awan for her infinite patience and unfailing sense of humour; to Sabah, Saimah, Alan, and Betty for allowing me to disrupt their kitchen for what must have seemed like eternity; to my mother for her typing skills and her invaluable food mixer; to Rory Mitchell for a constant supply of cakeboard; to Joanna Isles, Sally Burger, Jean Bolte, Angie Harwood, and Gwenda Evans for their support, encouragement, and bottles of wine at crucial moments; and to Pamela Todd in whose office it all started.